10 FEET TALL AND BULLETPROOF

10 FEET TALL AND BULLETPROOF

TRAVIS TRITT

and
MICHAEL BANE

WARNER BOOKS

A Time Warner Company

Grateful awknowledgment is given to use the following:
"Okie from Muskogee," by Merle Haggard and Roy Edward Burris. Copyright
© 1969 Tree Publishing Co., Inc. (All rights administered by Sony Music
Publishing, P.O. Box 1273, Nashville, TN 37202.)

Warner Books, Inc., 1271 Avenue of the Americas, New York, NY 10020

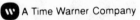 A Time Warner Company

Printed in the United States of America
First Printing: May 1994
10 9 8 7 6 5 4 3 2 1

Library of Congress Cataloging-in-Publication Data

Tritt, Travis.
10 feet tall and bulletproof : the Travis Tritt story / Travis Tritt
and Michael Bane.
p. cm.
ISBN 0-446-51847-6
1. Tritt, Travis. 2. Country musicians—United States—
Biography. I. Bane, Michael. II. Title. III. Title: Ten feet tall
and bulletproof.
ML420.T8136A3 1994
782.42'1642'092—dc20
[B]   93-49810
                          CIP
                          MN

Book design by Giorgetta Bell McRee

10 FEET TALL AND BULLETPROOF

Photo by Mills Fitzner.

Chapter 1

❀ ❀ ❀ ❀ ❀ ❀

Snap Your Fingers

It's cool to know how to snap your fingers.

I figured that out early, when I was about three years old.

Snap, snap, snap.

Positive reinforcement—"Look at Travis snap those fingers! That boy's going to sing for the Lord."

Snap, snap, snap.

Pretty soon, I found some words to add to the snap: Roger Miller's old "King of the Road."

Trailers for sale or rent . . .

"Look at little Travis sing! Isn't that just the cutest?"

Rooms to let, fifty cents . . .

"Here, here's a quarter. Go buy yourself some gum."

Travis Tritt, the musical prodigy of Marietta, Georgia, home of the Tritts. There's an elementary school named for my grandfather, half of a road, some other stuff. Marietta wasn't an Atlanta suburb thirty years ago—it was country. Out in the woods. A good place for a kid to grow up, and Tritts had been growing up there for generations. We did the same things all kids did then—pick on girls, build forts, be stupid. The only difference between me and my friends was that I was the kid who sang.

I was always walking around singing. If somebody asked, I'd snap my fingers and start right in: *Trailers for sale or rent . . .*

But the first time I remember being really bitten by the singing bug was in church, in Sunday school. We had a children's church, a kid's class, and the powers that be decided the kid's class should perform a song. The one chosen was "Everything Is Beautiful," and we had a month to rehearse. I was four years old.

We rehearsed ourselves about to death—little bitty kids, looked like a toy choir. The day we sang, though, stands out in my mind like it was yesterday. This was a very conservative Assembly of God church in Marietta, Georgia. That means you don't applaud after the hymns. Well, not only did the congregation applaud, but they gave us a standing ovation.

And I remember being just hooked, right then and there.

Standing there squirming while all those people stood up and applauded.

It felt good.

I got my first guitar, the guitar that I learned how to play on, when I was eight. It was a cheap Tempo guitar—when your eight-year-old tells you he's going to become a singer, so he needs a guitar, you don't exactly drop everything and rush to the music store. As I got better, I realized the old Tempo was only a notch better than those toy ukuleles with a hand crank on the side that play the Mouseketeer theme. But it was a guitar. And I could play it, thanks to one of those chord books—fingers here, strum. I was awful.

I came in from school every day and put my books away—if I'd brought books home, which, most of the time, I didn't. I'd throw them in the corner, run straight to my bedroom, lock the door, and get out my guitar. I knew every day that was how I was going to spend my time. Every waking hour that I possibly could I spent with the guitar, singing and playing, learning songs, learning new chords.

And standing in front of the mirror with a pencil, pretending it was a microphone.

One time I was standing there, crooning into my pencil, when I opened my eyes and saw my dad standing in the corner, just grinning. Shaking his head.

My fourth-grade class was assigned to write an essay on our favorite hobby. Mine was on playing the guitar. I got an "A" and an invitation to bring my guitar and play for the class sometime—my first real "gig."

I played "Annie's Song" and "King of the Road"—stick to your sure bets. And it worked. I got more "gigs": Other teachers would drop by to watch me play, then invite me to play for their classes. I got special permission to miss study hall every day and play for the other classes—my first "tour," I guess you could say. And every time I played, I knew I was good. I knew I *had* to be good for that many people in my school to ask me to play for them. Even if they didn't say another kind word about me, they'd admit that Travis Tritt could play.

When I was fourteen, my dad asked me what I wanted for Christmas. I said I want a twelve-string Epiphone or Alvarez or Gibson, a good guitar. I was, you'll notice, ready for this question.

"Son, I'm not getting you anything that makes noise," he replied. "Period. You spend too much time in your bedroom with your guitar now—it's all you do. It's not good, and I'm not going to encourage you. What else do you want?"

"I guess a .22 rifle," I said. Fourteen-year-olds are so good at hiding emotions. I knew he wanted me to get out of the house to learn how to do this, learn how to do that, work on cars, hunt, fish. I was completely resolved to the fact I was going to get a .22 rifle for Christmas.

A few weeks before Christmas, my dad told Mom to get ready, they were heading down to the music store.

"Why?" she asked.

"Travis is not going to be happy with anything but that damn guitar," he said. "We both know it, so we might as well get it for him."

It was one of the best Christmases I can remember, because the guitar was such a surprise and because it was what I really, really wanted. I still have it, and it's still a nice guitar. I just can't bring myself to get rid of guitars.

My mom's sister's husband, Sam Lockhart, was one of those guys who could play just about anything he picked up. He might not have been a virtuoso, but he could play a little bit of banjo, a little bit of fiddle, a little bit of piano, a little bit of guitar. He would work with me on the chords, show me new ones or correct me when I was chording wrong. He taught me "Wildwood Flower," then "Freight Train." When I was older, he introduced me to bluegrass festivals and other pickers. I loved it, loved it.

I was obsessed by the music. I played one season of Little League baseball. Absolutely stunk. Played two years of elementary school basketball. Stunk. Was never big enough for football. I hated sports, if sports meant I had to play.

Dad used to make us go out and work. Being the son of a farmer and growing up on the land, Dad didn't have a clue about how to plant a small garden. He planted enough vegetables to feed Ethiopia. There would be a garden as big as a small lake, three to four acres, rows of corn that seemed to me to go on as far as you could see. Then beans and okra and squash and all this stuff that I hated to eat. It's a miracle we survived our childhood.

I'd cuss that garden, and my dad would say, "Shut up and pick the beans!" Hoe, pick, can, play the guitar. Watch television and play the guitar. Mack Davis and Johnny Cash had television shows when I was growing up, and I studied them, their different styles. Spent a lot of hours in my room in front of a record player, rehearsing, making little tapes. I guess I just went crazy over the music. Didn't matter much what kind of music it was. All I could ever imagine myself doing was playing and singing, but that's easy to do when you're a kid. I discovered it got a lot harder as I went along.

Rio Diablo. (Photo courtesy of Kenny Rogers Productions, Inc.)

Chapter 2

❖ ❖ ❖ ❖ ❖ ❖ ❖

Boots and Hats and Cool

It was Big Time Love or, at the very least, Big Time Lust.

I was a junior in high school, bad dog, complete with long hair and cowboy boots, and Karen had just broken up with another guy she'd been dating. I got her phone number from a buddy of mine, and I called her, right after Christmas. Truth be told, I hadn't actually been cutting a swath through the girls.

I know you think of Georgia, you think hard-core rednecks in pickups and boots, but maybe we were just too damn close to Atlanta. For at least some people at my high school, country music was in, and I was in the center of it. I wore my boots and a cowboy hat, mostly to see how many classes I could get through before some teacher told me to shuck the hat or get out. That was the best part—getting up and walking out.

And while you're sauntering out the door, as cool as can be, the girls are looking at the football players and thinking that the guy in the boots and hat is a total geek.

I guess it was pretty much like any high school, except the one in *Beverly Hills 90210* maybe. There were jocks (they were the ones with the dates) and there were the druggies (they were the ones with the police records). There were the guys who wore black leather jackets and hung out in the smoking section in back of the school. And then there were guys like me, who spent time in recreational ed class (what is recreational ed, anyway?) throwing horseshoes.

Chewing tobacco and throwing horseshoes. Those are the guys that I hung with. I guess you could call us the redneck faction, although we didn't carry guns in the gun racks in the back of our trucks and didn't like to beat people up.

Just good ole boys, basically a little country.

Those were the kind of guys I ran with. You know, I was a fairly late bloomer in everything.

Picture this:

The school play is *Godspell*, and I'm doing some of the music for it, working out some bits on guitar or tinking on the piano.

Godspell—there goes my slot on the Grand Old Opry.

But it's music, and at least I'm getting recognized as a musician. Every day after school I was back there, working away. One afternoon I was really exhausted, and I sat down next to my English teacher, who, I suppose, should remain nameless. He was sipping from a Coke can, which he reached over and handed to me. Bad dog that I was, I took a big hit from the can, ended up with a mouthful of peppermint schnapps—honestly, my first drink of alcohol. Told you I was a late bloomer.

"Want one of your own?" he asked.

Oh man, I thought, this is so cool.

"Sure."

So he gets up, a little slowly, I think, and heads back to his office. When he comes back, he's got another Coke can, half filled with schnapps. He handed it to me, and I took it, real cool-like.

I got blown away, just wasted. And at that point— before I was dating Karen—I had actually managed to get a date, almost a girlfriend. And her dad had come to pick us up. She was in the play, too, and her dad was going to take us all out to a pizza dinner.

And I was just loaded by the time he got there.

It was the first time I had ever met him, and he was taking me and her and her two little brothers all out for pizza.

"Hard damned day," I said. "Shit, I never worked so damn hard in my life."

Her dad turned around and looked at me, sitting there smashed in the backseat, then drove on.

"No shit," I said cleverly.

He pulled the car over, and he turned around.

"Young man, if you're going to use that kind of language, you're not going to use it in my car and around my daughter," he said. "If you are, then you can get out and walk home, right here." I have never been more embarrassed.

Oh, well. So much for cool.

I did finally get a car. I bought a 1969 Rambler and paid $500 for it. It was blue—still is blue, sitting in my parents' backyard. Not a big market for used 1969 Ramblers. Friday nights, I'd call up a couple of buddies, and since I always looked older than I was, we'd get in the Rambler and cruise on down to the store and buy four of those big quarts of Pabst Blue Ribbon paint thinner.

And just go driving around . . . just stupid stuff . . . just go driving around, looking for trouble. I was a Mothers Against Drunk Driving nightmare, as stupid as only a kid can be.

So I call up this girl Karen, and for the life of me I can't remember where we went, but I do remember being smacked on the head with love, like the way only a seventeen-year-old can get smacked on the head with love. Everything was wonderful. This was the person I wanted to spend the rest of my life with. You know so much at seventeen.

Somewhere in the back of my head there was this dialogue going on: Get married . . . get an apartment . . . get out of the house . . . get a real job . . . get away from all this hassle at home. Nothing real loud yet, but it was definitely back there. In rural Georgia, that was the accepted path. When you couldn't live at home anymore, you got married, had a passel of kids, got a job down at this or that factory, and spent the rest of your life trying to figure out what went wrong. I saw my friends from high school graduate and head straightway on that path. And, for the life of me, I couldn't imagine anything different for me. I didn't even want anything different—yet.

Chapter 3

✸ ✸ ✸ ✸ ✸ ✸ ✸

A Joyful Noise

I have a good Christian raising. Fact is, a whole lot of prayers have been sent up on my behalf over the years, which is probably why I'm still around.

I grew up singing in church, which is a real Southern thing.

Everybody in the South grew up singing in church. My mother devoutly believed I should be in church every time its doors were open. She did her best to see to that.

One thing about the Assembly of God is they had great music. We had an organ and piano, then a guitarist, a bass guitar, and drums. Just about everything you wanted to play, you could play in church. We had a great music program. I dug that, because I could get up and sing solos by myself with just the guitar about every week.

I got pretty popular with the congregation, and I started getting requests. My dad, though, wasn't all that enthused.

"You know what they're training you to do, don't you?" he asked me one day. I didn't have a clue. "They're just training you to play those honky-tonks, you know."

That's a statement he made quite often over the years, and it turned out to be pretty much correct.

That's one of the reasons my mother was so opposed to my having a career in secular music, because she didn't want to prove my father right.

"Power in the Blood" was one of my favorite hymns. "Amazing Grace," of course. I used to do a song that wasn't in the hymnal: "In the Valley He Restored My Soul." Great song. I loved it, and the church loved it too. That tune got a lot of "Amens!" and the tears flowing.

A group of us played together in the church, playing I guess what you'd call contemporary Christian music. At times, there were as many as six or eight of us, sort of an orchestra.

We had a youth pastor who'd come in when there were only three or four of us. He was a great piano player, and he helped organize us a little bit better, took us one step further along.

I mention him because his story ended up in my song "Bible Belt." He's the preacher who ran away with the girl who played piano for the church. Both of them were married, but, as they say in country music, not to each other.

The youth choir went on a little field trip to Mississippi. When they got there, the youth pastor called the two leaders of the band in. Told them he wanted them to sing in the church tomorrow, then call the pastor back at home in Marietta to come pick them up. Next day, he and the girl had split, headed for parts unknown, although some of us suspected Las Vegas, to be married. Shook up our little community pretty heavily. I'd never seen anything like that.

It wasn't unusual for us to "tour," play other local churches. One Sunday we ended up at a black church.

I was a little bit nervous, because I didn't know how they were going to react to what we did. If we had gone in there and just sung "Amazing Grace, how sweet. . ." I probably wouldn't have worried. But we were writing our own stuff; a couple of guys in the band were writing most of the material. It sounded like rock music—acoustical, but definitely rock.

It was the greatest response we'd ever had. We were shocked. We went in, started playing, doing our thing, and people just went crazy. We were used to a white-people response—tap your foot, nod your head. But everyone was up dancing, getting with it, shouting, singing with you. Good singing, too.

Different than the way I was phrasing and singing.

After the first time, we started going to black churches whenever we could, and I listened. We were singing from the same hymnals, but we weren't singing the same songs. Black phrasing had all these bends and sweeps and curls, using your voice more like a musical instrument. When I tried it, I discovered something else very strange—I could sing that way. In fact, that was the way I was *supposed* to sing.

I could sing like that, and I knew a lot of people around me who couldn't. Plus, it just felt good, making your voice work that way. I'd entered a couple of talent contests prior to that, and I hadn't exactly been encouraged. The contests were always judged by choral instructors or music teachers or whatever, and they always told me I sang wrong.

"You slide up to your notes," they'd say.

"That's how you're supposed to sing," I'd think. I wanted to be George Jones, not Pavarotti. That black church was the first time I'd been "given permission" to sing the way I sang, and they loved it.

It gave me license. The next time we sang in a black church, my voice had a little more "soul." I was listening to Mahalia Jackson, Ray Charles, and Andre Crouch doing gospel tunes, trying to learn what they were doing. It started to change our music. One of our biggest requests was an Andre Crouch song called "Through It All." When I went back, I got even a bigger response than before.

I said, "Yeah, this is it."

There's such a close relationship between the church and music in the South. It's part of the Southern landscape—you sing in the church. The church was a very acceptable place for music. And not only that, you always felt good. Something about singing out in church, hearing all the voices together, made you feel good. You could walk around the house and sing to yourself all day long, but there's magic when you get in a choir with those harmonies and that energy bouncing around. It is inspirational—if you don't feel better than you did when you got there, then you probably shouldn't be going to start with. I always felt better after going to sing; a lot of time, I would have a whole lot rather been singing than listening to the sermon. But I enjoyed it. And I enjoyed the compliments. No doubt about that.

I definitely wasn't getting the compliments in school. In fact, my music teachers were giving me a hard time. There was one teacher who taught an elite chorus, and he'd been lobbying me all year to join up. I really wasn't interested, and I told him so. I also told him why—"I just don't want to sing the way you want me to sing."

Made him mad, I think.

I did the song "On the Willows," which is at the pivotal point of *Godspell*. It's a very sad moment; it's one of those times when everybody in the house cries. People came up to me at the end of the performance drying their eyes, thanking me.

The choral teacher came up to me after the show.

"You're still committed to not being in my chorus next year?" he said.

"Yessir."

"Too bad," he replied. "I still think I could teach you how to sing."

Photo by Alan Mayor.

Chapter 4

Songwriting 101

I wrote my first song for a little play I was in, probably in the third grade, but I don't remember what it was.

The first song that I remember really writing was called "Spend a Little Time," and—what a shock—it was about a girl. Aren't they all?

I was fourteen years old and dating a girl who was a high school senior, and I really thought that I was hot. Of course, I was dating her because she was about the only girl who had ever noticed I was alive.

I always felt, not like a nerd, but a little bit withdrawn. I tried sports for a while and was never any good at any of them, so I bailed out of that real quick. So while everybody and their brother was out making

17

the football team, I was in my room playing B. B. King or John Denver or James Taylor—whoever I could get hold of.

Anyway, I was dating this girl—an "older woman"—and she invited me to go with her on her senior trip to Gulf Shores, Alabama, in the heart of the Redneck Riviera.

I had visions of long walks on the beach, sunsets, all that cool stuff. How could it miss, a hot guy like me?

"What do you mean, you met someone?" I walked around, my hands stuffed in the pockets of my jeans. "We just got here."

She shrugged.

"He's a lifeguard," she said. Hell, that explained everything. "And he's a lot more interesting than you are."

I was devastated. Instant shambles. The biggest fool in Gulf Shores, Alabama.

It was already late, past midnight, and I headed out to the beach to walk, being that this seemed the acceptable thing to do for a shattered heart. I walked up and down, back and forth, and it didn't seem to do a damn bit of good. Finally, I arrived at a lifeguard tower, which I figured to be as good a place to sit as any, especially given my circumstances. Pretty soon it was 4 a.m.

"She could of at least spent a little time with me," I thought, and I liked that line. I rummaged around in my pockets and found a piece of a pencil and some scrap paper, and I just started writing. I didn't know what I was doing, except that I was hurting, and the writing seemed to help. The words came out easy, and in my head, I could hear the music that went along with the words. The whole process took about ten minutes. I was still stuck in Gulf Shores, Alabama, and I didn't have a girlfriend. But I did have a song, my first, which I called "Spend a Little Time."

I looked at the words I'd scribbled down there, and it was a little scary. I guess the first thought in my head was, "Where did *that* come from." Out of the night air somewhere? From space? From someplace inside my head, a place I previously wasn't aware of? Magic? I've written maybe 300 songs since that night, but I can still remember the wonder of those words on that paper. The song just came, arrived, like it had been there all along, waiting for me to find it. I'd lost a girlfriend, maybe, but I'd gained a life's work. Seems like a fair swap to me.

Once I got back to Marietta, I started playing "Spend a Little Time" for people. It took me a while to build up the nerve—I'd concentrated on that on the way home. It's easy to sit down in front of people and play your version of "Stairway to Heaven" or "Rocky Mountain High" or "The Thrill Is Gone," because there's no real emotional investment there. You're sort of the musical equivalent of a trained bear—it's not so much the quality of his trick, but the fact that he can do the trick at all.

With your own song, though, everything changes. Through whatever ether it arrived, a song you've written is part of you, a part of you that you're getting ready to unveil like this year's Chevy truck. The whole way coming home I just kept thinking, if they laugh, man, it's gonna make getting ditched by an older woman on the beach look like a day at the beach.

I got home and called some of my knock-around buddies, told them the good news and collected sympathy chips: Hey, how can a drugstore cowboy compete with a lifeguard? Everybody knows tans rot your brain. Then I asked a couple of them to come over in the evening, and maybe we'd goof around some. When they showed up, I hauled out the guitar.

"I wrote a song."

"Yeah, like 'I Wonder Who's Kissing Her Now?' "

Big laugh, so I just started playing, get through it real quick before I lost my nerve. When I finished, the response was respectful—something I didn't expect.

"Boy, Travis," said one of my buddies. "That's pretty good. Hell, that's a *real* song!"

Not so bad.

So I started playing it for people, and they liked it: "You know, you ought to write more stuff like that."

And the more people told me that, the more I thought, well, man, maybe I can write, and I gradually just started playing around with this and playing around with that. I really didn't know if I was a good writer or not, I guess, until much later down the road, when I met people in the industry. When you're playing little clubs and honky-tonks, playing for buddies and assorted relatives, you're always going to have some guy who, when you play one of your original tunes, is going to stumble to the stage and say, "Ah jess wanna say, son, that I thawt you was damn good, and you otta keep writin' them songs!"

Hell, I'll take the compliments where I can get them, but that same nagging voice in the back of my head said there were ten dozen kids who thought they could write and sing, and about nine dozen and eleven of them were very, very wrong.

I had relatives, people that I knew, acquaintances and friends of mine who were really not that good at

all, who stayed in the music business and attempted
to force some sort of break for themselves. Because
they believed every drunk who walked up and said,
"You're so good." I always kind of took that with a
grain of salt. Then I met Danny Davenport, a promotion man with Warner Bros. Records and the most
influential man in my career, and the first thing he
said was, "Hey, you know, your songs are good.
Your stuff is solid." It was a weight lifted off my soul.

Songwriting never comes easy, although sometimes the songs do. I'm not one of those songwriters
who can sit down at 8 a.m. and say, okay, let's turn
on the creative juices for the next six hours. I wish I
was; Lord knows it would be a lot easier. Instead, I
need turmoil; I need my heart and head churning.
When they've both churned enough, a song comes
out. For a long period of time after that first song, I'd
hear something on the radio, maybe by Hank, Jr., or
Waylon Jennings or the Eagles, and almost want to
slap my head like one of those cartoon characters.

Why didn't I write that?

I could have written that song.

That song is me!

That sounds like something I would have written. . . .

Only, of course, I didn't. I just couldn't come up
with songs like that—those guys made it seem so
simple. And every time I'd sit down to write a ballad,
it would come out sounding like John Denver or
James Taylor.

I discovered that I am the most unmethodical songwriter on the face of the planet.

Take a songwriter like Charlie Daniels. You can
give him the name of a place, a fictional place, Woolly

Swamp. You can give him the name of a fictional character, Lucius Clay, and you can say write me a song about that. And he'll come up with "The Legend of Woolly Swamp," with this whole story about this fictional place and this fictional time and this fictional event that took place there.

I have never been able to write that way, and I wish to God sometimes that I could, because I'd have a ton more material.

I write strictly from personal experiences, churned, like I said. Stuff I'm going through. Mostly love and romance, the acquiring of it and the loss of it. That tends to be a very popular subject with me.

I've been through a lot of that, both ends of that spectrum, so I can relate to that just about as well as anybody. Songs usually pop into my head all at one time, just like that first time on the Alabama beach. Sounds stupid, but it's like I have a radio in my head that is not always tuned in. But occasionally I'll be in the shower, or be riding the motorcycle, or doing something and be humming this little tune, or sometimes singing a whole verse and chorus and the whole nine yards.

And I'll stop and I'll think, now where did I hear that?

Who, you know, who did that song? And I'll start racking my brain, and I'll start realizing that's something that I heard on the internal radio. And then I just have to have enough sense to go in and write it down immediately.

I've lost more songs waking up in the middle of the night with this great idea and saying, "Man, this is wonderful." I'll sit there, and I'll think about it, and

I'll get this whole thing in my head, and I'll think it's wonderful.

I think, I'll write that down in the morning. And I go back to sleep.

Wrong. That radio in my head is notoriously fickle. So I've learned to either get up and write it down, or speak it into a tape recorder I keep by the bed, or those ideas are gone. But I'm very unmethodical, like I told you. I read an article on Johann Sebastian Bach, "I sit at the piano every morning at 9 a.m. in a position to receive . . ."

I think songs are a gift from God, and whether or not you're smart enough to be willing to accept them and take them when they come is up to you.

It's like that old Hank William story about "I'm So Lonesome I Could Cry," him asking for some paper, a napkin, anything, so he could get the words down before they evaporated, back to whatever ether they came from.

You know, I've written songs that I've agonized over for months. Gone back and rewritten the verse, rewritten the chorus, rewritten the whole thing. What I've learned is that your first impression is usually the best. And your first idea is usually your best impulse. If you have a sense or feel for what feels good to you, go with that.

Because there is no formula. I can't tell you how many people have told me "I'm Going to Be Somebody" would never be a hit record because it didn't rhyme. The song doesn't rhyme. It was still a hit. But there's enough "absolute–can't–miss–hit" formulas in Music City to fill a Broadman Hymnal. And those formulas are always imparted to you half in secret, like you need a decoder ring before you can really figure it out. Here's a "secret" formula—you've got to have the "hook," that little catchy part of the song that everyone will remember, in the first 30 seconds, or the song will never be a hit.

Okay, so here I am, Travis Tritt with a stopwatch. The only problem was that I wasn't sure what the hell they were talking about when they said "hook." Only hooks I was familiar with had to do with fish. I had to ask.

So here are all these guys, producers, writers, music people, sitting around saying, "I don't know, this sounds kind of like a hook to me."

For a while there, I thought maybe they were right, that I must be doing something wrong.

So I tried to change my style of writing, the way that I approached things, tried to be more methodical about it.

Well, it didn't work. Then I realized that these were the same people who'd told Randy Travis categorically that "On the Other Hand" would never be a hit record. It became one of the biggest hit records of the 1980s.

So what do they know? What do I know, for that matter? I gotta go with my gut, whatever feels good to me. There's a line from a Jimmy Buffet song I love: "Turning on the people, that's a mighty fine place to be/but if I spend all my time turning on the people/ then who's going to turn on me?"

I've got to move myself first before I can move other people. And I've always tried to go with my gut instinct, with whatever felt good to me. You know, I don't care whether the grammar is correct or that the proper secret formula is used, as long as it feels good to me. "Here's a Quarter" is probably going to go down—I hope—as a classic, and that's one of the simplest three-chord waltzes I've ever written. There are practically no words in the entire song that have more than two or three syllables. It's simple, very simple. And simple is what songwriting's all about.

Photo by Henry Diltz.

Chapter 5

❀ ❀ ❀ ❀ ❀ ❀ ❀

Blues Stay Away from Me

You hear more good music here in the Atlanta area than you hear in other cities. Especially Southern rock, Southern bar music, whatever you want to call it. The music doesn't change, but the niche it's stuffed into does. Sometimes it's classed as rock (say, the Allman Brothers in 1972), sometimes as country (Hank Williams, Jr., in 1986). But the music is very much the same, batted back and forth like a Ping Pong ball into different categories.

Southern rock has always been more than rock played down South, a whole that's greater than the sum of its parts. For me, Southern rock has always existed in that middle space between rhythm and blues and country—country blues you can dance to. It comes from growing up in the South, which—and I'll argue this with you even today—is simply different than other parts of the country. Back in school, when we were all young and dumb, we'd argue that, heck, it was because we'd lost a war. You don't have to look far around even Bright-New-City-of-the-New-South Atlanta to be reminded that once upon a time we got clobbered. That's pretty much bull, though, but it does bring us around to the central tension of Southern rock, the pull between black and white. North and west from Marietta are the foothills of the Smoky Mountains, where once the high, lonesome sound of the hills reigned supreme. Folk music that found its way over from England, from Ireland, from Scotland, was left to ferment in the isolation of the mountains.

Look immediately south from Marietta to Atlanta, or way west to Memphis, and you see the fields that spawned the chants that grew into the blues, hammered into the rhythm and blues of the cities.

So much came together in Georgia.

In Macon, Richard Penniman—Little Richard— filtered R&B through the rockabilly madness of Elvis Presley. James Brown, the Godfather of Soul, sang his unsanctified gospel, while Otis "Rockhouse" Redding sang a sweet soul music that had as much to do with white as black—remember, Otis's back-up musicians at Stax Records in Memphis were white.

And then there were the Allman Brothers.

The legendary Brothers, the ultimate fusion of rhythm and blues and country.

"People would come up and ask me how could white people play that way," Phil Walden, the founder of Macon's Capricorn Records and the man who helped launch the Brothers, once told an out-of-town writer. "Well, that's the only damn way they can play! They can't play Bach and 'Sentimental Journey'; that's not a reflection of their culture. Somebody asked Duane Allman why, when he was growing up in Daytona Beach, he and Gregg were always playing in black bands. Duane said, 'White kids surf; black kids play music.' "

I'd like to tell you that I bought the legendary "Filmore East" album when I was just a little kid, saved up my allowance money or something. Unfortunately, that's not true.

I got familiar with the Allman Brothers through "Midnight Rider," which had to be one of the greatest cuts ever—a scary song, like a Robert Johnson blues nightmare. It was so perfect, I couldn't believe what I was hearing. So I told a friend of mine that I'd heard this great cut, and he looked at me like I had just arrived from another, less-cool planet.

"It's the Allman Brothers," he said. "God, they've been around forever. Come over to my house, and I'll loan you some albums."

He gave me "Live at the Filmore East" and "Eat a Peach." What a shock! Here I was trying to invent the wheel all over again, and it was already down on record. Dickie Betts and Duane Allman playing together—I wore the grooves off my friend's albums, just listening and trying to figure out how to play that way.

I think of those records as the end of my musical innocence. I realized that I needed to do some catching up, not just listening to the radio. A lot of quick catching up, in a short period of time. I went back to 1968 and started listening. I listened to Creedence

Clearwater Revival and rock groups like Bachman Turner Overdrive. I listened to Southern rock icons like the Marshall Tucker Band and the Charlie Daniels Band. I listened to hippie music and Jimi Hendrix.

I was a little too young; I'd missed the 60s the first time, so I went back and caught up. Everything just sort of worked together. I always hung with an older crowd when I was growing up; I always felt more mature than most of the people my own age. I hung out with people who were four and five years older than me, and by doing that, I got a lot of varied influences with the music. I ended up with the musical taste of someone six to ten years older, because I went back in time. Most of the guys my age had no idea who I was listening to. They were listening to disco.

I didn't have a single white suit, no disco clothes whatsoever. But my high school actually taught a disco dance class. You know, in the sixth, seventh grade, they're teaching the Bus Stop and the Latin Hustle. I went out and bought the *Saturday Night Fever* soundtrack just like everybody else did, but somehow I could not relate.

The more I listened to Gregg Allman, the more I was drawn to black music. I began buying up blues albums, listening to Muddy Waters and early Ray Charles, following the musical trail back. I was already familiar with hard country music, the Merle Haggards and the Johnny Cashes and the high, lonesome sound, but country had turned sour at that point. It was soft, "countrypolitan," elevator music with strings. The more I listened to other forms, the more I was fascinated about how white and black linked together in the mongrel music of Southern rock.

I was completely disconnected from pop culture.

I didn't really catch back up until 1976–77, when albums like the Eagles's "Hotel California," "Rumors" by Fleetwood Mac, and Boston's first album were on the charts. There was just some great music that came out all at one time. So I was finally current again.

Thanks to the twelve-string guitar, I got to be hip again.

I'd learned how to play a twelve-string listening to old John Denver records. Plus Gordon Lightfoot and James Taylor, the whole folkie movement of the 1960s, where I'd been visiting. Fortunately a lot of the songs that were popular during the mid-1970s were songs that featured a twelve-string guitar. "More Than a Feeling," "Lady," even "Hotel California" started with a twelve-string guitar. I could sit down and play those things, so I could go to school and be kind of hip. That got me a few dates.

Country music bored me big time.

Willie Nelson was in his "Stardust" phase, and all of country music seemed to be following along. I always like to hear more up-tempo stuff, and it just wasn't on the radio.

A friend of mine's mother worked for a record label here, and one day she asked me over to listen to some new records—she got all these new albums before they were released.

She sat and played me a song, and I said, "Whoa! Who is that?"

Hank William, Jr., she told me.

I said, "As in Hank Williams, Sr.'s son?"

I had no idea who this guy was. God, it was great! I got a tape of that and realized that, once again, I was

31

behind. I started digging through country music with the same fervor I'd approached R&B. I rediscovered Waylon and Willie and began gathering up the music from Austin. Outlaw music.

I liked that phrase—outlaw music. For a kid in Georgia, it had just the right ring to it.

I started figuring out what all the ties were, that this all fits together. It started making sense then. You gotta put all the pieces together, and you start realizing who's connected to who, and who loves who, and, well, no wonder! You start reading album credits and you realize everybody's playing for everybody else. For the musicians, the "walls" between rock and country and R&B and blues were simply nonexistent, unimportant.

The musicians never saw a difference in what they were doing. Hank, Jr., could call up the greatest Southern rockers and ask them to play on his albums, and they'd be happy to. They knew who he was.

Rock musicians were very aware of what was going on. The lines were never drawn by the musicians.

I began, for the first time, to see my own music taking shape.

At least I knew what category to look for when I walked into a music store, instead of going through the "miscellaneous" bin—"The Best of Frank Sinatra" and, right behind that, Deep Purple.

Chapter 6

❋ ❋ ❋ ❋ ❋ ❋ ❋

Pickin' and Grinnin'

My uncle took me to my first bluegrass festival, and I was blown away. If you've never been to a bluegrass festival, imagine a small-scale Woodstock, only instead of all the music being up on stage, the whole audience is performing as well. Everywhere we walked there were clusters of people with guitars, fiddles, and mandolins, pickin' away. On stage, there were the "famous" people—the Lewis Family, Mac Wiseman, Curly Fox, J. D. Crowe, the New South— names that are familiar to bluegrass aficionados and pretty much no one else. To me, though, trying to get better on my guitar, the real music was in the field, in those little clusters of people. The cool thing about the festival was that I found out—to my surprise—that I could play bluegrass.

Bluegrass is a game of precision, of very precise instumentalists. You could be sloppy in rock 'n' roll, but you couldn't be sloppy in bluegrass. It simply wasn't tolerated. For a high school kid used to wowing people with long, distorted, sustained guitar licks, that precision came as something of a revelation.

Those master pickers pushed me, spurred me, to refine my own playing. I wanted to be able to pick like those guys. Get those clear bell-like sounds out of my own guitar.

Guess it's not much of a surprise that I got hooked on bluegrass festivals. I got hooked on the whole experience—hanging out in the parking lot, among the campers, picking with people who'd driven across the country. Camping out for two or three days and having some of the best pickin' in the world. We'd be standing in a circle pickin' and have somebody like Bill Monroe or Tony Rice or Jerry Douglas or Mark O'Conner—superstars in this world—step into the circle and join us. These cats would come walking up to your circle, with their fiddle or guitar of banjo or mandolin, you know, one or two or three o'clock in the morning, and just start playing. It was a humbling reminder of just how far I had to go. But it was also exhilarating—bluegrass music is like a big old Southern quilt. There a big patch of guitar, a big patch of mandolin, a big patch of fiddle, a big patch of banjo, a big patch of vocal, a big patch of bass. But just like a quilt is more than the patches that make up its top, bluegrass is really about the subtle intertwining of melodies, the threads that hold the quilt together. Sometimes, in the middle of the night, after pickin' all day until your fingers were numb, I'd imagine I could actually see those melodies, snaking out of Mark O'Conner's fiddle or Bill Monroe's mandolin, weaving around the more straightforward lines from us ordinary mortals. Maybe it was smoke from the campfires.

Also not surprisingly, I had to have my own bluegrass band.

And what's a bluegrass band without a banjo whiz? I lucked out—my school had a genuine banjo prodigy who had won a bunch of pickin' contests and everything. Told me later he just picked up a banjo and started playing it, like it had been lying around waiting for him to get started. I told him I didn't have that problem with a guitar.

He found out that I played, and I found out that he played, and we just got together, and said, "Well, who else do we know that picks?"

And, just like that, I had a band.

We went to bluegrass festivals to play with the bands, but they never allowed us to play on stage, because we had an electric bass. Bluegrass pickers are also very traditional, by the way. We weren't trying to make a political statement or anything. Our bass player couldn't afford a big old upright bass. Even if he could have, it would have been a major pain to lug that big old thing around school or to the parties we played. Electric basses had the twin benefits of being cheap and portable. Cooler-looking, too.

Eventually we entered a talent contest, but by then we'd already started mixing bluegrass and country.

Luckily, the group Alabama had made it big, and country bands, which had previously been looked on as lower than the proverbial snake's bell, had suddenly gotten cool. We came in second place doing "Momma, Don't Let Your Babies Grow Up to Be Cowboys." I've still got a tape of it somewhere, and I'm willing to pay money to see to it that it stays buried.

Where we actually honed our craft, though, was the little local rodeos. We'd all watched a couple of rodeos, so we'd figured out that the music was pretty much secondary. That's putting it real kindly. Inconsequential might be a better way of phrasing it.

The way it worked was simple: When the chute opened, you started playing like crazy people. Play fast and play hard until the bull or the bronco tossed the hapless rider into the stratosphere, or until the calf was roped, whatever. There was usually an eight-second time limit, unless they got thrown before then.

We go to be the best eight-second band in Georgia. We could go from zero to 150 mile-per-hour pickin' in nothing flat. And we could stop on a dime, WHAM, as soon as the cowboy hit the ground. Burn rubber, then slam on the brakes. We went a whole summer without ever finishing a song, but you'd be amazed at how much you can cram into eight seconds if you play real fast.

At the end of the night, you go play the dance, and everybody wants to clog. I came to have an absolute hatred for cloggers, simply because of the fact that if you're a bluegrass band, and you've got cloggers, what you end up doing is playing one song fast as hell—and you play it continuously for at least ten or fifteen minutes. Them cloggers, you know, can't do like a two-minute routine. From eight seconds to eight minutes.

But, I figured, that's show biz.

Me with Trisha Yearwood and our manager, Ken Kragen.
(Photo by Randee St. Nicholas.)

Chapter 7

❋ ❋ ❋ ❋ ❋ ❋ ❋

Ties That More or Less Bind

Oh God! Getting married!

The biggest cause of divorce in the world is marriage.

I was young, eighteen, and so was Karen, my high school sweetheart. The first person I fell in love with, the first person I had sex with. It is, unfortunately, an old story.

Looking back, more than anything else I wanted to get out of the house, get a break from the constant head-to-head battles with my parents.

Especially Dad. My parents had divorced when I was fifteen, then they remarried each other when I was eighteen. So they had just gotten back together, and I basically left a boy and came back a man. My dad and I didn't see eye to eye on a lot of things, and I wasn't as willing to give ground as I had been when my mom, my sister, and I left.

When we left, I didn't have a lot of choices. There was me, my mother, and my sister, and there wasn't anything to do but go to work.

Mother had been off the job market for a lot of years, and now she was in her forties, going back. She finally was able to get a job through a temporary agency working with Shell Oil, where she worked for quite a few years.

My first job was delivering furniture, a job I snagged when my mom, my sister, and I went to buy some furniture for the house we moved into after Dad left.

"Ah, Travis," said the store owner when we got there. "You gonna be working any this year?"

"Doin' what?"

"Well," he said, "I need somebody to help me deliver furniture."

So much for the "good old days" of pitching horseshoes after school. I hauled furniture for a while, mowed grass and cleaned up lawns, bagged groceries at a Food Giant, laid carpet, all those kinds of jobs you can get when you're fifteen years old and trying to help out.

Plus finance myself a little. That $500 Rambler still required insurance, and my guitar still needed strings. There wasn't anybody going to give it to me, because my mother simply didn't have it.

So the world changed.

I'd always been . . . I won't say sheltered, but I never had to go to work to help put food on the table. I worked, but it was always for extra cash, heck, money to blow. I guess I didn't realize how fragile the world really was.

So there was some leftover bitterness when we came back. Dad and I were butting heads consistently. There was no pleasing him, from my standpoint or from my mother's. My sister seemed to be the only one who could get along with him. Him, I think he was just bored with having been married all those years, bored with a couple of kids running around, and he just needed a vacation from all of us.

Who knows?

But I think when they got away from each other, they both started realizing the dating market is not exactly what it's cracked up to be. Maybe it was better to stay home, with someone you can rely on. Then they got back together, and they're still together.

Me, I bought Karen a ring for Christmas 1982, and we got married in September of the next year.

I bought the stone at a place that advertised they had the best prices in town, at least, one of the best *advertised* diamond places around. I went down and spent a bunch of time there talking to the guy, asking him all about color and cut and clarity, like I had a clue.

I didn't know anything about diamonds, still don't. I paid, I think, $1,500 for that ring. I paid forever on the thing—forever, never stopped, made a payment every month, coming in, you know, gotta pay on the right day.

My mom and dad had moved back in together, and the house my mother and my sister and myself had lived in was vacant, and I had a key. Handy thing to have when you're courting. So I proposed to Karen there, romantic soul that I was.

Big success.

She was all for it; her parents were all for it. My parents were completely against it, especially my dad, who had just one word: "Don't."

"It's not going to work," he said, adding that I was a bit . . . young. Of course, it just went in one ear and out the other, because everything he said at that point was negative.

Hell, I'd get married just to spite him.

So I did it, got married, and got six good months out of it. Moved all of fifteen minutes away from where I had been. Far enough that I didn't have Mom and Dad living in the backyard. Got a little one-bedroom apartment, and I bought all the old furniture from my mother to furnish the place. Got a "real" job working for a heating and air-conditioning company; Karen went to work for Burger King. Does this sound like a country song?

Being a late bloomer and waiting till I was eighteen before I slept with someone, the first six months was fine. Unfortunately, we had to come up for air sometime. And the more we came up for air, the less good things looked. We started realizing—surprise—that we weren't as compatible as we had thought we were.

It didn't help not having any money—never being able to go out, not even being able to afford a movie. Our primary source of entertainment became sitting around the apartment bickering at each other, watching the walls close in.

And there were the bills. Her parents had agreed to pay for this big, elaborate wedding—The Bride Wore White, you know. However, when the bills started coming, they came to me. My favorite was the bill for the $800 photo album, precious memories, which

I had to deal with on $210 a week take-home. My rent was $350 a month. No problem. At first, I considered eating the wedding album for a week, heck, a month. Then I briefly considered a raffle. Finally I just sat there and drank—cheap beer. Happy to have it.

My escape was my band, the same bunch of guys I used to play with in high school. We'd get together every Wednesday night—usually not in my apartment because the neighbors would complain, but at some-body's house. And we'd play. Occasionally we'd get a little gig to play a party here or a convention there, but very, very rarely. But I could tell that Karen didn't even like that smallest part of it. That's something I've wondered about for years. Was there an element of jealousy—that's me up there on the stage, getting all the attention, catching the eyes of other pretty girls. Or was it simply that you either love or hate the business—no middle ground. If you love it, there's no sacrifice too great; if you hate it, nothing about it even makes sense.

And that was a problem that grew and grew. We couldn't carry on a conversation five minutes without an argument. And all those arguments finally came down to just one: "If you don't like it, well, just pack up and move."

I came home at the end of one workday, and her mother had gotten this big Ryder truck and backed into the driveway of the house we were renting from my mom. They hauled away everything.

Of course, everything is a relative term, being as we didn't have much—it was a pots-and-pans di-vorce. But everything that was there was gone when I came home. The house was wide open, and very empty.

The cabinets were wide open; the front door was wide open, all the windows were opened—it looked ransacked!

Big time, big time pissed off. Called up her dad, threatened to go over to his house and, well, give him an attitude adjustment, but it was all just hot air.

Next time I saw her was in court.

The judge gave her everything she'd already taken, plus half of the equity in my truck as money, and I had to pay for six months of rehabilitative support, $150 a month or something like that, which was a pretty good chunk for me at the time. Plus, she got everything that she left with the exception of a couple pieces of furniture that I bought from my mother.

So I was really turned off marriage, but apparently not turned off bad enough 'cause I turned around and jumped right back into another one.

Did anyone here say country song?

Chapter 8

❋ ❋ ❋ ❋ ❋ ❋ ❋

Making Music for Money

*M*eet the Human Jukebox.

If you play every night, just yourself and acoustic guitar in those little clubs, you have to become the Human Jukebox. That means you've got to know everybody's songs, everything current on the radio. And, oh yeah, you might want to write some original material yourself. From "Sweet Baby James" to "Cat's in the Cradle" to "He Stopped Loving Her Today"—no continuity to it whatsoever. But I learned a lot from that.

There was this one big problem—my job. My career in the air-conditioner sales business. Between playing the clubs, booking and trying to manage myself, rehearsing, trying to write songs, and working the proverbial forty-hour week, time was running just a wee bit thin.

Well, I played the clubs for a while and worked the job during the day, too. Amazingly enough, I started to realize that I was making more money doing the club work than I was on my other job, the one I'd been working for several years. This is not a function of making it big on the club circuit, folks. This is more a function of a low-paying blue collar job. I had worked my way up from truck driver to manager and was working on the inside sales position, probably bringing down a couple of hundred after taxes. On the other side, I made about $300 a week, including tips, in the clubs. Cash.

The vice president of the company I worked for was a guitar player, too, an old rock and roller named Richard Laurens. He liked me, sat me down one day, and told me what a good worker I was. I finally decided I'd better level with him.

"Richard," I said, one afternoon after everyone had gone home, "I've got a few options I want to go over with you."

I was nervous as hell as he motioned me to sit down.

"I can stay here and try to work my way into that inside sales position," and he nodded. "Or I can quit and just play music for a living."

We sat there for a little bit, and he finally said, "I'd really hate to lose you, because you're a damn good worker, but if I had the opportunity to do what you're doing, what you have an opportunity to do right now, I probably would have to go out and pursue that dream."

He shrugged: "I kick myself, even though I'm very

successful in this business. I kick myself a lot now, because I didn't try when I could have."

Richard was in his mid-thirties, very much in tune with artists, and he loved to hear me play, loved the songs that I had written. And he said, "Look, I think you ought to go for it. You gotta do what makes you happy. You gotta get out and try, and if it doesn't work, you always have a place here."

I know it sounds silly, but he choked me up. He believed in me, didn't think I was some crazy kid. Didn't tell me to grow up. Those words meant as much to me as anything anybody had ever said. After years of working and playing, I was nearly beat to death. All I needed was that little encouragement.

I decided to play, period.

It was the toughest decision of my life. Then I had to build up nerve enough to tell my parents. My parents were a problem.

"Work," my dad said. "You're going to 'work' in the music business."

Work, he told me, was getting up at 7 a.m. and cranking up a truck or heading for a field. Work is something you did during the day that left you exhausted, with sweaty clothes and dirt under your fingernails. Just enough energy to eat supper and go to bed.

Guitar playing, that was what lazy people did while the men worked, people who most of the time ended up drunk, broke, or in jail, or various combinations of those three things.

"Son," he said, "I know you don't want to hear me say this, but you've got a better chance of becoming President of the United States than of becoming a so-called 'star.' That's hard, but that's the way it is. And those other long-hairs you're hanging with, they just want to take your money. Grow up, boy!"

When you work the clubs you start your first set at about 8 p.m. You play five sets a night and get off around 2 a.m. By the time you get through with all the stuff you gotta get done, which usually involves tearing the equipment down and loading it up, you get home at 4 a.m., so you sleep until noon the next day.

My dad would sometimes call about 9 in the morning to see if I was up, and it would just infuriate him to "catch" me still in bed, wasting away doing nothing. But I was paying my bills, and that's one thing I always used as my defense.

My mom was just as upset, but for different reasons.

"Travis, you're a good Christian boy," she'd begin, and I knew what was coming. It didn't originate with my mom—the break between gospel, the music of the church, and blues, the music of the Devil, was as old as the South. I just didn't figure on having to deal with it so frequently in my parents' kitchen. "A Christian doesn't belong in the bars. If you want to sing, you can sing the Lord's music."

She raised me in church. The first place I ever sang was in church, and her basic idea was that singing was a God-given talent, a fact I never argued. It's a point that I understood but never acted on. I also knew that to make it in the business, I couldn't just do gospel.

You've got to play the clubs; you've got to play those honky-tonks. What I found out was that you didn't necessarily have to be part of it just because you are playing around a bunch of drunks. You don't have to become one of them.

I did, because what you know and what you do isn't always the same thing. When it comes right down to it, both of my parents were a little right. They'd heard tons of stories about everybody from Elvis Presley to George Jones and all the things famous entertainers were going through. In the back of their minds, even if they were thinking maybe I did have a shot, they were thinking that the consequences of success could be pretty high. Who can blame them for being concerned about their son.

And they were right, 'cause I did get caught up in that trap for a while. Drinking real heavy. And doing those little pills to keep me awake and going. It's hard not to.

Fortunately I found out what a detriment that was once things started getting off the ground with Warner Brothers. The liquor and drugs put up a barrier between me being what I was and me being the best that I could possibly be, which was always my intention.

And I remembered thinking thoughout the entire time that if my competition was the band down the street, then that's as good as I'll ever be. My competition was not the band playing at the honky-tonk down the road; my competition was Hank Williams, Jr., and George Jones and George Strait and Randy Travis. Those were the people that I had to compete with, and I could never, never let that slip out of my mind.

My friends would have thought I was crazy, except, at that point, I didn't have many personal friends. I made a lot of acquaintances through the clubs that I played in, and all of those people were very supportive. It's very, very easy to rearrange the people that are closest to you so that you have more supporters than naysayers. I *needed* people to come up and tell me, "Hey, you're good. You need to hang in with this."

It's easy to find people who'll tell you what you can't do. Too easy. And it doesn't matter whether it's in the guise of "You stink" or "I'm only telling you this for your own good." The result is exactly the same. If you stop to listen to those people, you're going to find yourself stuck in place, unable to move. The more radical your dreams, the more likely people are to step on them, hard.

I was already getting that from my parents, so I definitely didn't need that from people around me. When I found myself surrounded by people like that, I cut them off and went on.

There were seven major clubs around town that you could count on for a booking. And I don't know why, but fate always seemed to play in my favor. I'd have a two-week booking and no idea where the next meal was coming from, nothing to back it up with. And, always, right at the last minute, on the last night, some guy would call up, or we'd get in touch with somebody and they'd say, "I hear you're doing pretty good stuff over there at that club." Amazingly—to me—I went very, very few weeks without work.

Here's the way it works:

The whole booking process is very subtle—you call up the owner of a club and tell him you're the greatest act in the history of country music, which he knows is bull, and that, if he should hire you, about 10,000 of your closest friends will be there every night to support you, buying liquor like there was no tomorrow. Okay, maybe it's a little more subtle than that, but there were times when my pitch was pretty close to that.

Then it's usually an audition—"Come in on such-and-such an afternoon, set up your equipment, and play for me." Or come in one night and play for free and see how the crowd accepts you. That's usually what the bookings are based on.

I started out doing it that way, the way it had always been done, and what I found was that club owners were some of the biggest liars that I'd dealt with anywhere. Here's the way it *really* worked: They'd say something like, "Okay, tell you what I'm gonna do. We'll book you for two weeks, and we're gonna pay you $350 per week for five nights a week, five or six sets a night." At the end of four days, the club owner would come to me and say something like, "Well, it's just not working out like we thought it was going to, you're not drawing in as many people as we thought you would, so we're gonna end this booking right now . . ." Did I mention that we got paid at the end of the week, after five nights?

Or I'd go in to get paid on Saturday night expecting the $350, and they'd hand me $150 and say, "That's all we're gonna do." What could I do?

So I started typing up contracts and having the club owner sign them. I felt better, until I realized the things didn't mean spit. The club owners pulled the same thing, and when I whipped out the signed contract, the response was, "So sue me."

When I started out as a single act, I wanted to be different from the run-of-the-mill guys with a stool and an acoustic guitar. I'd seen a local act who played standing up, and I thought that really added to his

stage presence. He also had a little drum machine—
Japanese electronics have changed everything—and I
thought that helped. So I adopted the stand-up-and-
sing pose and added my own drum machine. I also
added up my pennies and went out and bought a twin
reverb amp and my first Fender Stratocaster guitar.
I'd never played an electric guitar in my life, but what
the heck. A Strat was—and is, in my book—the cool-
est electric guitar in the world. I figured I'd give 'em
a show.

As soon as I showed up with the Strat and amps,
the club owners would start to sweat bullets.

"Now we want you to play real soft music for the
first two sets," they said, "because you got people
eating."

Actually, they wanted you to play that way all
night.

Okay. But after the dinner crowd had gone home
to sleep it off, I was planning to rock. Try to get their
attention, because the club audience was not there to
hear me. They could care less if I was replaced by a
loud radio or a "real" jukebox or a dancing bear.
They're in the club to drink, have a good time, drink,
talk to their buddies, drink, meet members of the
opposite sex they're not married to, drink, and avoid
members of the opposite sex they are married to. I
wanted them to notice me, so I got a 50-foot cord
between the Strat and the amp, and by the third or
fourth set, I was doing "Johnny B. Goode" from the
top of one of the tables.

I got fired from a lot of gigs.

Chapter 9

* * * * * * *

You're Fired!

Go out and buy an amp, speakers, and a Strat when you don't have any money; that'll put a dent in the old budget. A tremendous dent. Sure, it was an investment in myself, but that didn't make it hurt any less. I bought better-than-average sound equipment, because I wanted to sound as good as I possibly could. I wanted to stick out as something different, something unique, above and beyond all the other solo acts.

And in one way it worked. I was definitely getting people's attention and drawing people in. On the other hand, I was still getting fired a lot.

I remember one club in Marietta called Wall Street. It was a real nice place, a dinner club—tablecloths, real silver on the tables, glass-topped tables, polished wooden floors, nice bar in the middle.

I'm sitting over in the corner, like one of the potted plants.

As a matter of fact, there was a potted plant right next to me. I bought a couple of little spotlights to hang from the ceiling and had my own little gig going. Every night it was something different—turn it down, or this is not the Omni, or you can't jump up on tabletops, you can't do "Johnny B. Goode," you can't do this, you can't do that, this is not the crowd.

It was a little hard for me to understand, since before I started the weekend crowds were averaging a whopping twenty to twenty-five people sitting around sipping white wine. After I started, there would be a line waiting out the door to come in. Maybe the house wine had gotten better, but I suspected they were coming to see me play. I was bringing people in.

I couldn't understand what the problem was, why the club owner wasn't appreciating the standing-room-only crowds.

Nope—our way or the highway.

If people knew I was singing at the club, they'd come. Of course, then it was my fault when things were slack. I found it very hard to get up and play exactly forty-five minutes, take a precise fifteen-minute break and then start back right on the hour when there was nobody in there to play to. So I'd leave and walk outside or get in my car and drive down to another club on my break to see what was going on. I never sat in with anybody else, but I listened to other bands to see what people were doing. And I got fired for doing that. I got fired for all kinds of crazy things.

The first time I was fired was from Wall Street. There were two business partners who owned Chico Dills (the first place I played) and Wall Street. And they had a disagreement. One guy took Chico Dills and the other bought out Wall Street. So when I got fired from Wall Street, I went back to Chico Dills and said, "Hey, I'd like to come back and do some things over here," and I talked them into letting me come back and work. It was just that kind of thing, back and forth, and there were a couple of other clubs that I would also try to work around so that I had at least four or five bases that I could move from. Here two weeks and there two weeks. I did that for quite a while—it felt like an eternity, believe me.

I pretty much had a reputation for being a pain in the ass, you know, hard to deal with, that kind of thing.

The type of sleazeball who would actually type up his own contract.

I was never good at seeing something that I felt was wrong and keeping my mouth shut. A perfect example of that is the first year that Dollywood, Dolly Parton's amusement park in Tennessee, opened. There was a guy, Dave Mack, working with us who had some connections with the people at Dollywood.

He showed up one night with a proposal: "I got you a great booking, Travis. Dollywood's opening up, and I got it set where you'll go up there for a week in July and play on the opening stage as people come into the park. You're gonna play a bunch of sets during the day, and it'll be great exposure for you—plus you get into the talent contest that they're having."

All right! We loaded up my pickup truck with my gear, drove all the way up to Sevierville, which is strategically located near the end of the world. Dave said, "I'll meet you. I'll take you over to Dollywood and introduce you to all the people you need to be introduced to."

All the motel he booked us in needed to be perfect was a big sign in front that said "Bates Motel." After waiting for hours, we gave up—Dave wasn't coming. Finally I took the initiative, got into the pickup truck, and drove over to Dollywood to find out what was going on.

I went through I don't know how many people with walkie-talkies trying to find somebody who was in a position of authority and who had some vague idea of what I was supposed to be doing. Finally I found somebody, but I didn't like what I found out. Yes, I would be playing on the opening stage, but I was alternating with another act. So what I had to do was play one forty-five-minute set, then break down all the equipment for the other band. Forty-five minutes later, do it all again.

Well, it was the middle of July and 104 degrees out on the asphalt. The park had a dress code—T-shirts were inappropriate. You had to wear long-sleeved shirts with collars and cowboy boots and jeans. And I had quite a bit of equipment, and nobody with me but my wife. I knew that there was no way in the world I could tear all that stuff down in between sets, and even if I could, I'd be so sweaty, I wouldn't look or feel like performing for anybody.

That night, back at the motel, we still hadn't heard from Dave. About 11:30, he called and said "Come down to the pool. I need to talk to you about what you're doing."

I went down to the pool, and he filled me in on

the requirements for the next day's talent contest—including no sound check—and that he was really counting on me not to screw up.

Right.

I lasted one set the next day. I went storming around the park until I found him at one of the restaurants, having lunch with three or four of his promoter friends.

"This is bullshit," I said, declining the offer to sit. "If this is the best you can do, I'm going back to Georgia. You and Dollywood can kiss my ass."

After much soothing of feelings, they moved me to a stage that wasn't even open yet in the middle of the park, down in a hole, all roped off. Nobody knew I was there, but I could stay on the stage for the rest of the week.

When I got back home, I wrote a letter to the people in charge of the bookings at the park and told them how unprofessional I thought that thing was to be carrying the name of a star like Dolly Parton. I wondered if Dolly knew what was going on in that park.

I got a letter back suggesting that if I was going to make it in this business, then I was going to have to learn not to be so difficult and roll with the punches and do this and do that.

I did a lot of ass kissing—at least, things I thought were ass kissing—in the early stages, and went along with it; I tried not to rock too many boats. I didn't intentionally want to get a rep for being hard to deal with. But it was all one more frustration that I didn't need at the time.

On the definite plus side, I learned how to put together a band, which is largely by fortuitous accident and blind-ass good luck. There was a club in town called the Buckboard—still there—that had a house band led by a guy named A. J. O'Brien. There was a one-night-a-week jam night, and musicians would just stop in and pick—I've done my share there. A.J. mentioned that a harmonica player named Jimmy Joe Ruggiere had been coming around. Said the harp player had spent some time in Key West, then drifted on to Dallas, and finally ended up in Atlanta. It just so happened I needed a harmonica player, so Jimmy Joe and I started playing together. In fact, he was such a good draw that I talked one of the club owners into paying both of us, so we became a duo.

Then I found Wendel Cox. He'd actually been mentioned to me years before, when I first got started, by a friend of mine, who told me "this little cat"—Wendel was about seventeen years old at the time—was the hottest guitar player he'd ever heard. Three years later, I run into the same guy, and he's still pitching the same guitarist, who can at least now order his own drinks. So Jimmy Joe and I added him to the lineup.

I had a bass player, but after eight months he'd had to bail out. Jon Bonnette, house painter by day, bassist extraordinaire by night, signed on for the full ride. Tim Passmore was playing fiddle in a little club in Blue Ridge, Georgia, working as a fireman to make a living. He was so hot, we drafted him right out of the fire department.

I was doing all my own booking and my own management, such as it was. There was no one else to do it, and no money to hire.

Chapter 10

❀ ❀ ❀ ❀ ❀ ❀ ❀

The Album from Hell

My first recording project resembled a fire drill.

I had no money to do a professional tape anywhere. Studio time costs money—a lot of money. But if you're going to get anywhere in the business, a tape is exactly what you need to have. Tapes are the jungle drums of the record business, and when you're just starting out, you need a "demo tape," a demonstration tape to show what you can do. It used to be that those tapes could be recorded on a cheap cassette player and bundled off to Nashville. Then jump back while you turn into a star. A couple of major factors changed all that.

The first is simple competition. Music isn't so different from selling cars. When only a relatively few people were sending in tapes, the tapes usually got listened to, and the quality of the tape wasn't a big concern. With the incredible boom in country music, that number of tapes flowing into record company offices has turned into a staggering torrent, enough to keep everybody in Nashville busy listening to tapes for the next few years.

The second is the advent of "home" recording studios. Guys with a few thousand dollars and the patience of saints could sit in their attics and crank out higher and higher quality demo tapes. The standard kept rising, and I knew if I was going to have a chance, I needed a professional tape.

All I lacked was the requisite amount of professional money.

An electrician friend of mine was wiring up a home studio in some record company promotion man's house in Atlanta, and he had a brainstorm. Bet he could talk this record guy into letting me use the studio for free or for a little electrician work. I figured it couldn't hurt, but the homeowner, Danny Davenport, a promotional guy for Warner Bros. Records, was less than enthused. Finally he agreed, as long as we didn't wreck the place.

My friend—he was the closest thing I had to a record producer—set everything up, and I came in with my guitar and recorded three songs, including "Spend a Little Time."

"How do I sound?" I asked my friend the electrician.

"Great," he said. "I guess."

About halfway through the second song, the owner of the studio, Danny Davenport, walked in. At first, he looked like somebody who smelled something bad—I guess it was the idea of seeing an electrician and a totally inexperienced singer use his studio. After a couple of minutes, though, he sat down and listened.

When I finished, he took the mike from my friend.

"Ah, uh, Travis, did you write that song?" he asked.

I nodded.

"Where have you been all my life?" he said, and I started feeling pretty excited. "We need to talk."

Danny Davenport—sometimes Fate walks into our lives wearing the strangest disguises. Here was this big, shambling hulk of a man, long hair, scraggly beard, looking at me like I might be a particularly interesting insect. I knew he was a promotion man for Warner Bros. Promotion men are that invisible level of the music business, the people who directly contact radio stations, who work to get a record on the air. What I didn't know at the time was how well respected he was in the music business. He had a reputation for honesty, not "crying wolf"—calling Warner Bros. every week to tell them about the "next big thing" he'd heard in some bar.

I also didn't know that he was fiercely loyal to his friends, and that once he committed to a project, he was as tough as an old bulldog until it got done. What I also didn't know was that Danny Davenport held the key to my future, the key to unlocking my dreams.

I leveled with Danny—I'd been beating my head against the wall and getting nothing but headaches. I told him about the clubs, the songwriting, the dreams.

"So why don't we make an album?" he said. "We can use it as a demo and sell it at your gigs."

So we decided to make a record, overlooking the fact that none of us were producers or engineers, or even had a clue about how a record was made. Hey, we've got an old woodshed studio! Let's do our own musical! So every Sunday and Monday night, my only two nights off, we'd hit it. And almost every Sunday and Monday night the tape recorder would break, the wiring would short out, the soundboard would be sounding "a little hinky." Bad karma, flowing like water.

Sometimes literally.

The studio was just the back of Danny's garage, a little bitty room that was originally intended to be used for storage. Danny had put a glass window in it, then built another tiny little room as the control room. There wasn't room enough in the "performing room" for the electronic drum set, so we put it in the only other enclosed room we had, the toilet.

Preparing to record meant unplugging the old Coke machine, which made a lot of racket, shutting off the air-conditioner, which was the only thing that made the garage habitable, and making one last visit to the bathroom. Then we'd all go into our respective rooms and turn into artists, musicians, and producers— sometimes all at the same time.

"I don't know, Travis, but it just doesn't reach me," Danny was fond of saying. I seriously thought about reaching through the glass for him every time he said that. In fact, none of us had a clue. He didn't always know how to tell me what he was looking for. I didn't know what I was looking for, and some idiot had always just flushed the toilet.

I figured on a couple of months of Sundays and Mondays, but at the six-month point, I was beginning to worry. When we crossed the one-year threshold, I was wondering if this project would ever end, and

Danny was wondering if his newfound "star" was already developing a "star" attitude.

Aside from the fact that we were suffering from two-night-a-week cabin fever, a more deadly disease than you'd imagine, my music was changing. The process of sitting in the studio and working out songs was helping me focus on what I really wanted to do. When you start out as a performer, you are the sum of your influences. You might do ballads like James Taylor or up-tempo stuff like Waylon Jennings. Ideally, if you're going to progress in both the artistic and business sense, you've got to become more than the sum of your influences, another one of those easier-said-than-done tricks. I don't think you can force it. You can hear it in the evolution of artists like Waylon Jennings or Hank Williams, Jr. In the early albums, you hear the artist being bounced from producer to producer, from style to style. What I think of as the "sounds like" theory—"Do something that sounds like . . ." But early in their careers, you suddenly hear an album that has the artist in control—Waylon's "Dreamin' My Dreams" or Hank, Jr.'s "Friends" album. At that exact point, they go from potential to real.

At first I thought that might be like a lightning strike—Bang, you're there! But about midway through the Endless Album, I wrote a song called "Gambler's Blues," and I knew when I wrote it that it was pointing the way for me to go. It just felt right, a lot more connected to Southern rock than my earlier stuff. The more I played it, the more I realized that this was a side of me that was going to have to be nurtured if my music was going to mean anything at all.

Damned if I wasn't going to have a little outlaw edge after all.

It took us forever, but what we ended up with was an album of eleven songs titled *Proud of the Country*, most of which I had written. Those recordings became the foundation that my style and sound have been built on. In spite of the numerous mistakes we made, I am proud of what we accomplished in that little woodshed studio.

It was a first for me and a first for Danny and a first for everyone else, too. I never did learn how to patch *this* into *that* and so forth. As a matter of fact, even now, I'm looking into a little portable studio, and my requirements are simple—"Get me something that's so easy that any fool can hit play, record, rewind, fast forward," 'cause I still don't have any idea.

Chapter 11

❀ ❀ ❀ ❀ ❀ ❀ ❀

Second Time Around

How could this happen?

I just got through a really bad divorce, and I'm married again, almost within the year?

Well, at least she moved in with me within the year. We lived together for about a year and a half, and then we were married.

Wait, I can explain everything—she was an older woman, more mature (than me), smart, petite—what can I say, completely the opposite from my first wife. And me, I managed not to learn anything.

Jodi was her name. She was working as a waitress and racking pool tables at Miss Kitty's, one of Atlanta's premier nightclubs, long before they ever agreed to let me on the stage. I was hanging out,

Meeting People, you understand. Actually drinking and shooting pool, but Meeting People sounds ever so much better.

But while I'm sipping and deciding about my future, I start hitting on the waitress. I've got this little button on the bus now, and it reads, "My life is like a string of country songs." I wouldn't dispute that in the least. So you've got a lonely, bored country boy, beer, Jim Beam, and a beautiful waitress. Twang, twang.

And that's when I made the decision to start playing the clubs. But I was just getting started, and I met her, and she was extremely supportive.

First, she'd just bring me a drink and rack my table for me. Later, I came in not to shoot pool, but to get her to rack the table. I was twenty-one or twenty-two, old enough to know better, but too stupid to care. She was thirty-three. After a while, I convinced her I was a real musician, and she'd come over to the little clubs I was playing, to watch me perform.

When I asked her out the first time, she said she didn't go out with younger men.

Wave that ole red flag in front of a bull, sport.

I sat one night at the bar and just talked to her for hours and hours and hours, and, finally, when I asked her again to go out, she said sure.

A lot of times she'd come out to the club where I was playing and watch me play my last set. And then we'd go to breakfast together or something. Jodi was renting a room from a lady, and I said, "Why don't you just move in with me?" We lived together, got married and stayed married about four years—it was a lot better than the first time, a lot better.

I really thought this would be the one. I guess everyone looks out there and sees that proverbial white house with the picket fence. But forces—not the least of which was my persistent immaturity—were already at work to collapse the dream.

Okay, forget the sinister forces. I take a lot of the blame for the second divorce. She was supportive of the business, helped me get bookings, took care of a lot of the business; she was there at most of the gigs, with me during the day, with me at night. It seemed to work.

And then came the road.

Things were finally starting to jump—a record company was interested in me; the band had finally come together; the energy was really getting good. And we were traveling—a week and a half in North Carolina, three days in Orlando, a week in Macon, jumping all over the South. You call; we come.

But there was still no money, and I couldn't afford to take Jodi with me. We're all jammed into cars, sleeping in the same motel room or on someone's floor. No place for a woman, I rationalized. So she stayed at home, and because she had pretty much closed her friendships down and adopted all of my friends, her life was centered around me.

My life began to center around the road. I'd meet with record label people; I'd work on writing new songs; I'd talk with booking agent people, trying to lay the groundwork for my dreams. I'd get done with my sets, then go out with this record executive, or this guy, or that guy, and have drinks and bullshit about future plans, blah, blah.

That accomplished two things. First of all, there really wasn't the opportunity to miss her as much as she was missing me. Jodi was sitting there looking at four walls, wondering what I was doing right then. In truth, about the only time I really missed her was when I was by myself. When all the *other* stuff was over with.

The second thing was the same old problem. I'd come home after ten days, and all I wanted to do was park my behind on the couch with the remote control in one hand and Domino's Pizza's number in the other. She, on the other hand, had been sitting home for ten days, and she wanted to go out.

Sensitive person that I was, I just said no, I'm not going. Not surprisingly, she started going on her own.

The word is immaturity, and I wish I had a better excuse. I was just at the point of getting caught up in the business, riding the tiger. It was like being caught in a whirlwind. The bars are seductive, even now. And nothing seems as immediate as a man who tells you he knows the secret of making your dreams real.

You know, you have to buckle your seatbelt. A few months before, I couldn't get my phone to ring to save my life. All of a sudden, it never seemed to stop ringing. Now everybody's wanting to talk to you all at once . . . things are starting to pop . . . we're talking about a possible record deal . . . the record contract is signed . . . we're talking about a release date . . . now we're talking about, well, maybe we need to talk about managers . . . and maybe we need to talk about this . . . and all these people calling and . . . there's stuff happening . . . it's the buildup just before the big explosion, before the volcano erupts.

And at that point, I became very, very—probably a third *very*—selfish and very self-focused. And I think probably it was a little bit more than she could take. If I'd been a little more mature, maybe we could have sat down and talked about it. If cows had wings, they could fly, too.

The anger set in first, before we could talk. Maybe because we didn't talk about it immediately, anger and resentment just started building. By the time it was something that should be, must be, talked about, it was such a sore subject that nobody could discuss it.

There wasn't a whole lot of shouting and stuff. Toward the very end, yes, but not a whole lot.

She just felt like I just left her behind, which is what I had done.

I was getting a new life, and she was part of the old one.

I was so caught up in everything that was going on at the time, and it wasn't all one-sided, it does take two, you know. I think from her side too there was a lot of . . . I don't know . . . At that point, I don't know if you're ever really prepared for what's going to happen. Neither one of us knew. This whirlwind came in and took over, and once things started popping, it happened really fast. Up until that point, she'd been like my booking agent and my . . . not really manager, but *involved.*

When Warner Bros. stepped in with their professional people, there wasn't room for Jodi anymore. She was being pushed to one side, and that led to a lot of anger and a lot of jealousy. She didn't feel like I was sensitive to her, and I didn't feel like she was sensitive to me. And neither of us had a clue.

We separated. I started a sexual relationship with another woman, and that put the icing on the cake. I was thinking (when I was thinking), "Hell, nothing can be salvaged anyway. It's just a matter of going through the ritual of signing the papers."

So I signed the papers. Attorneys were calling me night and day, using words like "record royalties" and "future earnings," going after anything and everything they could think of. I couldn't believe my own bitterness. "This is what it all comes down to," I kept thinking. "Doesn't matter where you start or what you want or desire. It all comes down to attorneys in the middle of the night."

I finally had to get people from Warner Bros. to say, look, she had nothing to do with his career, his being signed by this record label. I'd met Danny Davenport before I met Jodi, and he had everything to do with me getting the record deal.

My second divorce was final in August, and "Country Club" came out in September.

We're not friends.

The funny thing in both of my relationships is that after they were over with, I never once wanted to go back. I guess I thought if I'm going to get burned, it's not going to be by the same person twice. But in both cases, they've called me or written me letters or come to see me up within days of the divorce proceedings, wanting to get back together. It would have been a big mistake.

I wrote "Here's a Quarter" the night I got my divorce papers.

My second divorce, at twenty-seven years old. Sheriff knocks at the door, presents me with the second set of divorce papers that I've gotten in what I think of as a relatively short life.

And I'm thinking, this is a drag.

What is wrong with me that I can't stay in a relationship with people who love me? Is it that I'm so focused on the music that I'm willing to sacrifice whatever I have to in order to be a success, or am I just your basic asshole?

I was really, spectacularly, world-class depressed that night. Here's the funny thing: The divorce papers were in my hand. I was getting ready to sign them, and she called me.

Blood-in-the-streets divorce, dueling lawyers sneaking around, threats, finally getting ready to sign the papers and get on with it after an out-of-court settlement that took more legal power than negotiating a treaty with a banana republic. And she called me.

"You know," she said, "maybe this is a mistake. Maybe we ought to try to get back together." Far too much water had gone under the bridge for that.

"You made this decision," I said. "You've taken it this far. You filed for the divorce. You moved out. It's done. There's no turning back."

Lots of tears from both ends of the telephone.

Just a little irony here.

I told myself I was going to do one of two things: Either I was going to go out, get extremely drunk, and wake up the next day with a terrible hangover and the same old problems, or maybe, just maybe, I could stay home and do something constructive.

Unfortunately I had no idea what that was going to be. I'd considered the possibility of breaking up the furniture, but I just didn't have that much to break up.

So I did what I always do—go get the guitar as an "adult pacifier."

I started playing some chords and adding lines, just

71

to make me feel better before I signed those papers. Pretty soon I started writing seriously. The whole song took less than fifteen minutes. When I got done, I just cracked up laughing. All the venom, all the anger, had been translated into "Here's a Quarter," and I felt better than I had in months. The song was going to be my personal talisman, something to cheer me up whenever I got down. I never intended to play it for anyone else. Whenever I started feeling depressed about the circumstances, I'd say, well, she called me back; she's wanting to come back now that she sees what she's missing out on. So, na na na. There's my little song. I'd play it to myself and I'd chuckle about it and I'd go on with my day.

It took me years to be able to play that song in front of an audience.

Chapter 12

✷ ✷ ✷ ✷ ✷ ✷ ✷

Crazy, Crazy Times

So I swore off marriage forever.

I figured, you know, this isn't working, so I thought I'd try a new track—I just went absolutely crazy on the road.

Let me define absolutely crazy for you:

Basically, sleep with anything that threw itself in my direction. I was young, twenty-seven years old. I was a rising country music singer. I was on the road. I had gorgeous women throwing themselves at me all the time. And I was single again, and I had sworn off marriage.

Yes, ma'am, Travis is here.

Fantasy time!

I went through my middle-age crazies at twenty-seven.

I indulged in everything that my position allowed me, which was pretty much everything. This is one of those puzzling phenomena, you know. While I was growing up and dating, I always felt pretty awkward. I didn't have much of a gift of gab at any point. I could never just walk up to somebody, especially a female-type somebody, in a bar and just start talking. I'd open my mouth and seize up. I felt pretty insecure about myself. I've said it a million times—my guitar and my music introduced me to every person I ever met. Every girl I ever met, especially.

All of a sudden, women were throwing themselves at me.

I'd never been an athlete, wasn't a jock, wasn't in a position where people were lining up to get a date with Travis. And now, there were all these women!

Women with careers. Educated women. Women that I would have died for a date with. Only they didn't want a date with me, just sex. No involvement at all, other than the obvious, physical involvement. No long-term possibilities, just like, "We want to sleep with a star. Tomorrow morning, I'm out of here." And I go to the next one, the next night.

Attractive women. Female attention—it was shocking for me. I didn't even have to work for it. Get up on stage, play my songs, do my show, and when I'm done at the end of the night, here they were.

Point my finger and pick—no conversation, no drinks, no, "I love you forever." They didn't exactly come for a relationship.

And I'm not going to lie to you. I enjoyed it, for a while. For about five or six months, I absolutely loved

it, because it was a new thing for me, something that had never happened to me before. And I'm not going to apologize to you. It is not something I'm proud of, but let he who is without immaturity cast the first stone.

One night on the bus, after about five months of "Pleased to meet you, I'm Travis," about 3 a.m. I had a couple of major thoughts.

You can have all the sex you want, I thought, *and it's 3 a.m., and there's not one soul of the opposite sex who really gives a damn whether you live or die.* There was no one to pick up the phone and talk to.

The thought about "die" rung another, long-overdue bell.

Man, this is crazy, I thought. *I'm going to end up killing myself out here doing this.*

Literally.

As soon as I got back home, I got a blood test. Then I waited around for a couple of days for the results, my stomach in knots and my brain going stupid, stupid, stupid. Negative. I started getting blood tests done every two months, just to check and make sure.

I would not, I knew, be the first singer to die while experimenting with the attention.

I guess anytime you're experimenting with something new, you tend to overindulge. It's that way with anything—alcohol, sex, drugs, whatever. And then I think "whatever" becomes a very tired subject very soon. The new wears off, and it just doesn't make a whole lot of sense anymore.

I don't claim intelligence, maybe just dumb luck, but I've always been able to realize when I was involved in something that would eventually get me. And I've always been able to get out before it did.

So I started to rein things in.

I pulled back. It's an experience I've had, and I can go on.

The real question, I think, is how can a traveling performer have a real relationship? You're thinking that should be pretty easy, being up in the spotlights and all. But that makes it all the harder—you can't date fans, because fans look at you as larger than life. It's not a lot of fun to go out on a date with someone who's staring at you like she's waiting for you to walk across the swimming pool.

Fans fall in love with the image. You can call it a cliché all you want, but they're not interested in the real person, in the real me. They don't want to get to know the real person, because if you get to know the real person, you can't be a fan any longer. And I couldn't help thinking that if I wasn't in the position I was in, this woman wouldn't be sitting across from me, smiling. I doubt very seriously that if I was still loading trucks off the dock, many women would drive by the dock and throw panties at me. You know, not too many guys standing on warehouse docks get underwear thrown at them on a regular basis. But I get on stage every night, and that happens. So here's the conundrum—are you supposed to date people who don't like you, who think your music is for hicks and degenerates? Or are you supposed to date music business people, so you can have penetrating lunches in Nashville and discuss the position of your latest single on the Billboard charts?

Robin Williams once gave a great description of how this image thing is, and how people fall in love with images. It's like going to Mardi Gras and seeing all of these beautiful, elaborate papier-mâché heads

going down the street. They're gorgeous, vibrant, and beautiful things. Very aggressive-looking things, and underneath them, there might be this very shy, withdrawn little person.

So you find yourself at the point of wanting somebody you can sit down and have a conversation with, who doesn't even know a sentence that begins with, "Ah, I can't believe I'm sitting here talking to . . ." At that point, I started looking for what was real, and that proved harder than I'd ever imagined.

I put up a huge wall after my last divorce. It's still there, mostly. It's real tough to break down. I said you become immediately skeptical of everyone, and that sounds like a real negative thing. I guess it is. But once you've been shopped around like a piece of meat through the system, pretty soon you start believing that everybody is just looking for the prime cut.

When you start out, you have to put up with it, because it's the way the machine works. But when you get popular enough, and you don't have to put up with it anymore, it's like . . . it's almost like a rubber band stretched out and then released.

But you end up cutting out the legitimate feelings, too, and people who care for you. That is the thing I fear most, alienating the one who really loves me for me.

I'd love to have kids. I just wish that there was some way that you could get a money-back guarantee with your relationship.

If you don't work on a relationship every day, you've lost it. It'll slip away from you. The trick is preventing the career from stealing away the time you should be devoting to that relationship.

When you become a public figure, the public owns

you, at least a chunk of you. That's a fact. If you plan to be in this business, that's just a fact you're going to accept right off the bat. I've seen a lot of artists over the last few years, toured with some—if I called their names you'd say, oh, yeah, I remember that guy or that girl. They were talented enough, but they weren't willing to be this public.

And if you're not willing to do that right off the bat, then you might as well step aside, regardless of how talented you are, because there is always going to be somebody else coming up behind you who is as talented and will be willing to be that public.

I accepted that very easily before I even signed on the dotted line for the record deal. I understood from the start that if I should become a success, I would belong to my fans. I would be a public person. I would owe a certain amount of my lifestyle, or all of my lifestyle, to those people who help make it happen.

Did I want that? Weighing out the positives and the negatives, the answer was yes.

There is a price to pay. If you're going to be a lawyer, you've got seven years of school. If you're going to be a doctor, you've got ten years of school. There's a price to pay for achieving success in any field. If you're going to be in the music business and you're going to be successful, the fact is that you give away a large percentage of your private life.

And you come to guard the private part that's left. It becomes almost sacred, the one shred of normalcy that you have left. This is the anchor that keeps me sane. Your privacy becomes so small, yet so important that you guard it with everything you've got. This is why I eventually came to build a huge dirt wall between my farm and my neighbors', after they built a "Tritt Viewing Platform," complete with camera tripods, overlooking my backyard and swimming pool. Ah, well . . .

When I finally signed with Warner Bros. Records, they offered me stage passes for all their other acts that came through town. So whenever I wasn't working, I was backstage, watching artists like Hank Williams, Jr., and Randy Travis. It was obvious that once you got the success, you had to cough up the price of that success, which was the end of your privacy.

I was backstage at a Hank, Jr., concert, the first time I'd taken advantage of those backstage passes, and I couldn't figure out who the heck all the people were. I finally asked somebody, and the answer was, basically, people who wanted something from Hank, whether it was their picture taken with him or to get him to invest in a business deal.

It amazed me how many people were milling around, wanting to get to Hank, Jr., as if he was going to have time to see the hordes and perform as well. I didn't see how he was going to have enough time to see the people he saw. And Hank saw very few people.

I knew what I was setting myself up for, but, hey, I get to catch the winning touchdown pass from the Super Bowl every day of my life. I get to be the hero every day, and it's fun.

If you look, and it doesn't take very much digging, you can find the negative in anything. Where the challenge comes is in finding the positives and making the positives outweigh the negatives. I realize this sounds a little Pollyanna for a country music singer, and I'll admit, I wasn't always a particularly positive person.

When I was playing in the clubs, trying to get something off the ground and getting fired from all the places that I was playing in, I was anything but positive. You develop this theory of your art, which goes something like, "You know, I'm going to make it in this business, and I'm going to come back and nail you with it." I actually told one club owner that when he fired me. Got all puffed up and said, real country-like, "Tell you what I'm going to do. I'm going to make it someday, and whether you like it or not, one of these days your jukebox is going to be full of my records, because people are absolutely going to demand that you play them. And I'm going to get me the biggest, nicest Silver Eagle bus I possibly can, and I'm going to pull in your parking lot, and I'm going to dump the sewage tanks right smack-dab in the middle of your lot and salute you as I drive off."

He laughed at me. Well, maybe it was immature, but every time the bus passes his place the thought does still cross my mind.

But negatives are a kind of cancer. If you let it continue, even though you've got all this great stuff going on around you, you're not happy. You wake up every day in a bad mood, and you're not happy with anything. And you should be, you know. Here I was, an angry young man. I had everything in the world I ever wanted, was selling tons of records, was financially stable for the rest of my life.

What was I mad about? I started realizing, very slowly, that life's too short to go through it unhappy, especially when you've got no reason to be unhappy. There wasn't a specific turning point, no revelation. Just a steady dawning that the bile I was feeling was misplaced. I looked around me and saw a lot of other artists with the same bile. Put us in a room, man, and we could bitch the night away.

It starts in just a very small way. Then before you know it, everything's a negative, nothing's good about this business. It sucks, the tour sucks, the road sucks. Then you think about, wait a minute, two years ago we were playing in a little pissant honky-tonk bar someplace, where you did good if you had twenty or twenty-five people to play for and they gave a gun or a knife to everybody at the front door so they might be equal. Loaded and unloaded all your own equipment; you were basically just a peon with a guitar. And now you walk out on stage and play for 10,000 people, and they love you.

Get serious here.

I think I grew up an awful lot in that short period of time. I knew both sides of the coin—what it was like to live without money, and what it was like to live with it. I knew what it was like to go through a phase where you had virtually no attention and I knew what it was like to be adored. I knew what it was like to never have sexual attention; I knew what it was like to have women lined up in front of the hotel. There were no myths anymore.

The question was what was I going to do with all the information? Pretty good question.

Me with Buck Owens. *(Photo by Rick Moxley.)*

Chapter 13

✵ ✵ ✵ ✵ ✵ ✵ ✵

Honky-Tonk Heroes

Pay close attention here.

I'm going to reveal to you the Three Unmutable, Always True Laws of Honky-Tonk:

One—Eighty-nine percent of all bar fights are over women.

Two—Always make friends with the bouncer.

Three—No one can fight when you're playing "Silent Night."

A girl walked into a bar I was playing and sat down, close to my little toy stage. She was fairly attractive, blonde, cutoff jeans, nothing out of the ordinary. I was playing along, Mr. Jukebox, when she took her top off. Kind of like she was hot or something. Like she always took her top off in bars. Maybe she did.

No good, I thought as I glanced down at her now-bare bosoms, can come of this. I started trying to work out exactly what my exit plan would be when the situation re: Ms. Topless became untenable. The most amazing thing to me was that it took a good twenty minutes before the first fight broke out—I think she was surrounded by very large admirers. Once the fight broke out, though, it was a gem—tables falling, fists flying, bottles breaking. I don't recall exactly what happened to the blonde. I did what I always did—grabbed my guitar and headed for the hills.

Bar fights are tough on guitars. They fall down, the neck cracks. There goes your old favorite. Harder on acoustic guitars than an old Stratocaster. You could probably chop wood with an old Strat. Still, prevention, as they say, is the best cure.

The first thing you do, if you don't do anything else, is you make a damn good friend out of the bouncer. You find out who that bouncer is and you buy him drinks if you can afford it (even if you can't). Introduce him to some good-looking girl you know. Be his pal. You do something for that bouncer, because that's the guy who's going to save your life if something breaks out. If he doesn't particularly care for you, you're in a bad, bad way, because you're up there, defenseless.

At that point your guitars and your microphone stands serve two functions—music makers and de facto weapons. You have to remember that you can grab the end of the guitar by the head stock and swing in your basic baseball-bat stroke. Have I done that? Yep. Welcome to Honky-Tonk World.

The trick is to know how to retreat. Like when the

two huge, freight-train-sized cousins decided to shoot themselves at the 'tonk in south Georgia. They were regulars, and they were fighting—over a woman, I do believe. They were also situated at a table just in front of the stage. It's hard not to notice two planetary bodies in coveralls going at it ten feet from your face. When one of those planets reached inside his coveralls—time to go, boys and girls.

Where do I go? 'Cause there's not a dressing room. There's not a separate bathroom, not a quiet place that you can hide in. I'd plotted it out in advance, just like you always have to do. How do I get from this point to the exit sign? You work that out in your head as soon as you take the gig.

I stood up and walked rapidly to the bar and out of there.

The cousins? They shot each other in the parking lot. I guess that is the way Hank done it.

"Silent Night," though, proved to be my all-time lifesaver. Just when things started getting out of hand, when bikers were reaching for their pool cues and rednecks were headed to the gun rack, I'd start playing "Silent Night." It could be the middle of July—I didn't care. All of a sudden, these big old guys with their fists cocked would look at me bleary-eyed and lower their hands. Sometimes—I swear—they'd even start crying, standing there watching me sweat and play Christmas carols.

Some nights, though, there was no way to win.

I had an old lady one night, a little bitty defenseless drunk lady, sweet-looking little grandma, who came up to the stage with a request. I was sitting on a stool on the edge of my stage, about a six-inch step up. My microphone stand was in front of me. Grandma didn't want to just give me the request, she wanted to whisper it in my ear. So I was sitting there, got the guitar, got the microphone stand, and she reached up, grabbed me by my collar to pull me close to her so she could whisper this request into my ear. She didn't realize that there was a step up, which she missed. Grandma fell backward, pulling me, my guitar, my guitar stand, my microphone stand, my stool, and everything else right into the middle of the floor, on top of her. The edge of my guitar cut her face. I'm apologizing, trying to get up. She's bleeding. The crowd is laughing. What do you do for an encore?

Here's a corollary to the Three Unmutable Rules: Play whatever the hell they want; nobody knows the words anyway.

"Play 'Lovin' Her'!"

"Well, sir, just tell me the title . . ."

" 'Lovin' Her'! 'Lovin' Her'! You damn well played it last night!"

"Lovin' her was easier . . ."

"Damn it! That's not it! 'Lovin' Her,' you damn fool."

Try "He Stopped Lovin' Her Today."

When in doubt, fake 'em out. I probably wrote more verses to Eric Clapton's "Cocaine" off the top of my head than anybody else on earth. It was easy to play—one of the first songs I learned—and simple, one sentence with a rhyme: "If you want to get down, get down on the ground, cocaine." I knew that first line. I also knew there were about twenty verses after that, and I didn't know a single one of them. But I could rhyme like a crazy man, then end with a powerful "cocaine." I could do almost a whole set on just that song. I even got requests for it. Sorry, Eric.

One day I got this great idea to insure my equipment against damage. I started calling insurance companies and explained that I was in business, the music business, and wanted to insure the tools of my trade. That got a good laugh. About a week after that, the tools of my trade got scattered all over the place, speakers turned over, everything tossed around. The fight came up quicker than a prairie fire, and I was lucky to get myself off the stage, forget the equipment. I came back, hooked everything up, and it still worked.

But usually the folks in the crowd were happy because they were drunk and didn't know the difference. I was always pretty good at hearing a song and being able to play it quickly, because I spent a lot of time listening to the radio. I'd tape a song off the radio and listen to it over and over again, figuring out the chording, the words, the arrangement, then slot the song into my set.

Sometimes, when the crowd was pretty good, I'd slip in one of my own songs. I might get by with playing one a night, but no more than that. I had a strategy, though, for the 'tonks. Play good, and get more and more people in until they outnumbered the regular bar denizens. Eventually it would reach a critical mass, when even the regular customers would start listening to the music rather than beating each other on the head.

All of a sudden you've got people in there who are actually paying attention to the music, actually there to enjoy the performance. Once you get those people in, everything works. You can perform without keeping a wary eye on the exit sign, in case you've got to make a run for it. Then you can start doing more of your stuff.

That's usually when I got fired.

But, heck, it's a strange business. You learn how to deal with any circumstance that comes up, because you've pretty much seen it all. I've seen people shot, stabbed, beat up, run over, arrested, passed-out drunk, doped up, having heart attacks, going into seizures, women in labor—all during my shows. Occasionally I even got to play some music.

Chapter 14

✤ ✤ ✤ ✤ ✤ ✤ ✤

"Just Sign the Paper..."

Right after I quit my day job, I started working for a local singles act hero, Bo Griner. I'd watch him, try to learn stuff from him. And I did learn a lot. So when Bo decided to go to Music City itself, Nashville, he thought it'd be a good idea for me to tag along and record "Spend a Little Time." This is before the Album from Hell.

Okay, I thought that was pretty cool. And there were fantasies, you know, along the lines of, "My God! A music genius, trapped in Marietta, Georgia, and we were lucky enough to capture him on tape!"

So I went along with him just to see what the deal was all about. The first thing we did when we got to town was meet with a "producer," who stuck a piece of paper in front of me and explained that I needed to sign that before I'd be allowed to record. Yessireee, just call me old country Travis. I signed the paper. I found out later that by signing the paper, I gave that song away, for perpetuity, I believe it read, forever. Someone else is the publisher. Welcome to Music City, greenhorn.

We stayed at a motel out by the railroad, which was loud (a minus) and really cheap (a big plus). One of the drawbacks of the two of us being in Music City was that we didn't have a dime between us, and clubs cost money. So on my first visit to Nashville, I stayed in the motel room and watched television all day long. We did spend a lot of time walking around at night, figuring to spot big stars. We didn't see a one, and, according to the Nashville *Tennessean*, none were playing in town. Weird business, I thought, when you go to the home of country music and can't see anybody.

So we went in and cut my song that wasn't my song anymore. I didn't know that my hero had put up his own money or had a record deal, I just enjoyed being there. When we got to my song, I thought I'd put my two cents in. In a nice way, the producer told me to shut up.

Chapter 15

✸ ✸ ✸ ✸ ✸ ✸ ✸

Meeting and Greeting

I had to have a game plan, if I could just figure out what the game was.

I saw people like Bo Griner, who did his own album, brought a bunch of record label people in to listen to it and took for granted that they'd love it, sign the singer and he'd be a star, presto chango.

How could they not like it? It was his lifework.

They hated it. Presto chango, everything stays the same-o.

It, being the music business, just doesn't work that way. There's a system that you have to go through, and its rules are not spelled out. Everybody comes at it in a different way.

Danny Davenport had enough credibility after his

twenty years in the business to call in some chips. He had a reputation for not "crying wolf," and he believed that we had a shot.

We had to find a plan and work that plan. When you run into the inevitable period of time when the plan's not working, you drink. You get frustrated and say, "I'm going to quit."

The brickwall factor I found at the club level is always there—it just moved up to a higher echelon. From club owners to managers to businesspeople to executives in the recording industry.

You spend years doing the right thing to prepare yourself to take advantage of luck when it finally happens.

Like I said—it's not so much a lightning strike as being around in the thunderstorm, holding a metal pole—a whole sequence of events that you do correctly so that when an opportunity presents itself, you can move.

Like playing the clubs, getting to a point where I was getting a lot of attention from record labels and there was starting to be a "buzz" about this guy Travis Tritt. Instead of a series of lightning strikes, I'd moved through a series of plateaus. Move up to one more. It's a domino effect.

"Look guys," Danny told the president and head operating guys at Warner Bros./Nashville, "I've been in this business twenty years, and I've never asked you for anything. I'm asking you to listen to this and give me your opinion." He played *Proud of the Country*.

That wasn't met with enthusiasm—Nashville has the equivalent of a "Not Invented Here" syndrome. Record companies believe they are machines that un-

cover hidden talent or find a kernel of talent and nur-
ture it into superstardom. They have had some luck
with that policy but, as a rule, they haven't been
overly successful in the discovery and nurturing end
of the business. Some of the hottest acts in country
music have come in over the transom or had to beat
down the door before a record company "noticed"
them. It takes a Danny Davenport to be able to pick
up the phone and call in a marker. This isn't bull, by
the way. Once you call in a marker, it's gone forever.
If the heavyweights at Warner Bros. had played the
record and not heard anything, Danny's stock would
have dropped to nothing in about the same amount
of time it takes to pop the top off a bottle of beer.

Things fell where they did because we had a precon-
ceived idea. Danny and I would sit up nights and
nights on end, talking about what our moves should
be if this happened or that happened. Talking about
what happened to other artists when they took this or
that path.

And even with all that planning, the cold, hard
truths of the music business still come around real
fast. I figured, up until the time the first single came
out, that, man, you get a hit single, everybody becomes millionaires. You get a label deal and you get
a hit single, bang, instant millionaire. Buy two or
three buses, head out on tour, have more hit records,
and everything just kind of falls into place. As a result
of having hit records, you get good reviews and
more, better, bigger gigs. You didn't even have to
pass "Go" to collect the $200.

Surprise. It just doesn't work that way.

Danny got us signed to a singles, not an album deal,
after months of deliberation. It works this way: The

record company signs us to record six songs, of which they'll release three singles. If one of those three singles hits, well, the company reconsiders the deal. If it doesn't, you're out of here. Go home.

I got lucky again. We picked the right material and had a hit right off the bat. But I've said for years that you only get one shot at that first impression. And I always tried to make sure that whatever my first impression was, it ended up, "Hey, this kid's got something here." It was a tricky thing. I wanted that album deal right off the bat. I saw people like Clint Black and Garth Brooks getting album deals out of the box, which is how rock music has always been. But that's not the way country worked, they told me. Randy Travis started with a singles deal. Dwight Yoakam started with a singles deal. So Travis Tritt was going to start with a singles deal.

No problem, I said. Could cost me a lot of initial momentum, I added to myself.

Chapter 16

✦ ✦ ✦ ✦ ✦ ✦ ✦

"Country Club"

*W*e were on our way back from a showcase performance—not a big audience, but mostly movers and
shakers—in Nashville, at a little restaurant that had
been turned into a high-ceiling listening room.
"Country Club," my first song, had been on the
charts for several weeks and was climbing. People
came up to me constantly and said, "I'm hearing your
stuff, man, and it sounds great."

I thanked them. I wish I'd heard it. But so far,
despite vast amounts of dial twisting, nada. Believe
me, I was listening all the time. The band and I had
rented two vans, big old Ford Econolines with bench
seating, and we were cruising down the interstate on
the way home. It had been a good showcase—we'd

been allowed to invite a lot of people in, and the house had been rocking.

We'd started into the foothills of the Smokies, where the Nashville country stations begin to break up, when the deejay said, "Don't go away. After the break, that much-requested song from newcomer Travis Tritt, 'Country Club.' "

"Pull over!" I shouted to the driver.

He hit the breaks, and we skidded to the side of the road.

"We can't lose this radio station!"

We sat there and waited, and, finally, the opening bars of "Country Club."

We all just went crazy, like a bunch of kids, high-fiving each other and shouting. We'd waited an awful long time for that moment.

The pendulum had swung from bad times to good times. I had done what I had said I was going to do. You can say what you wanted to, you could argue with how I got there, you could bitch, moan, or whatever, but the naysayers didn't mean anything anymore, because I had done what I had said I was going to do.

The future, all of a sudden, looked bright. After being in one spot and spinning your wheels for as long as I did, it was nice to be moving, even if it was just a couple of inches at a time.

It had been a grim few months since recording the single. I guess after we cut the single, we thought everything would miraculously change, kind of like being annointed by this big musical god. We had a Recording Contract, a Single, we weren't just some local bar band scraping to get by.

Except that as soon as we finished cutting "Country

Club," we headed back to Marietta to resume the life of some local bar band scraping to get by. The release date of "Country Club" kept getting pushed further and further out.

We'd be playing Miss Kitty's in Atlanta, our "home" club, and when we'd get to "Country Club" we'd dutifully say, "Our new Warner Brothers record, soon to be released."

At first, that got us some cheers. After a few months, we said that and a voice in the back shouted, "Bullshit!"

That hurt. We all began to get more and more frustrated, tempers flaring. Wait. Wait. Wait. Wait for the break. Wait for the session. Wait for the release. There was also this sick feeling in the pit of the stomach that maybe the whole thing was some huge scam I just hadn't been able to figure out yet, that there were crowds of people hollering "bullshit!" behind my back. The guy in the audience was just the outward manifestation.

The hardest thing to overcome was the fear of failure, because of what failure carries with it. You might say, "Well, if you fail, you just turn around, and go back and sell air-conditioning parts." And I knew that's probably what would have happened. But it's not that simple. Failure means that you have to go back to all of your friends who you told you were going to try to do this, go back with your tail tucked between your legs.

I'm far too proud a person, for better or for worse, to be able to handle that well. I'm so competitive—I don't accept defeat well at all. I'd been dealing with that fear for a long time. There were times when I numbed myself to it, just stayed drunk. Drink heavily and you don't think about it as much. You're numb to everything. There were times when Danny Davenport was my only thread. But we laid the groundwork. For so long, that's all it seemed like it would ever be.

We'd cut "Country Club" in late 1988, aiming at a Halloween release.

Months passed. The song was finally released in September 1989.

The next hurdle was video, more specifically, the fact that Warner Bros. didn't, as a rule, do videos of new artists. Videos have become the 800-pound gorilla of the recording industry. It's no secret that videos have changed rock—made it more visual, more susceptible to "look-good" pressures. That's the way country music is going. To an extent, it's good, because it gives the fans a "sampler" of the artist, helps answer Question One, which is, "Who is this guy, anyway?" I think that's particularly important for a new artist, because nobody knows who you are. More importantly, though, a video for a new artist offers another no-cost way for the public to get to know you. It's hard to overstate the importance of this in a world of $20 concert tickets and $14 CDs. In days past, you could hear a new act on the radio, buy the album for a few bucks, then see that act at a small club for $5 or so—I did it a hundred times growing up. With such a huge proliferation of new acts, though, and the escalation of even small club prices and CDs, you could go broke trying to keep track of country music.

Enter the videos, a second screening before you shell out for the concert ticket. Sounds good, looks cool, where's my wallet?

Videos also help airplay. I don't know how many radio station disk jockeys told me later, "We were getting calls and requests for that song before we even had it in the studio because of the video."

All I did was insist that we had to have a video on the first single. You would think I had asked for Dolly Parton to be kicked in as a bonus on my contract. The words "we've never done that" and "that's not how we do things around here" probably ought to be etched in marble over most record companies' portals.

In spite of everything, we got the video.

I had a huge amount of creative control. I got to pick where we filmed—Miss Kitty's in Atlanta—and then sit down and be quiet until they were ready for me. I got the video. I figured there was a time to shoot off my mouth and a time to shut up. It was shut-up time.

Filming that video was a little like watching paint dry, only less exciting. It's almost like being back at the rodeo—singing a snatch of song over and over again, striking the right pose again and again. But it worked. I didn't look like one of the "hats," the country music newcomers who all looked like they walked out of an ad for Rodeo Cologne for men.

I managed to catch some of the channel surfers— "We just happened to tune past your video, man, and we didn't even know what it was, maybe MTV. . . . We saw this guy in leather pants and long hair who looked like a rock star . . ." Well, the song wasn't rock. Nothing about it is rock. But I was no "hat act," and this video bore that out. I was something different.

Photo by Mills Fitzner.

Chapter 17

❀ ❀ ❀ ❀ ❀ ❀ ❀

Gettin' Ready for the Big Time

So I had the hit record I had been dreaming of. "Country Club" was moving up the charts. I was ready to be a millionaire (aren't we all?). Instead, I discovered I was getting ready to get poorer.

In the clubs, I had been doing all my own bookings. Now I had to get an agent. I discovered that I couldn't book myself into places I wanted to get booked. It's kind of a twist on the old "I wouldn't become a member of any club that would have me as a member" line. If I was big enough to play these places, I was big enough to have someone else make the telephone call.

I also needed a manager, since Danny Davenport and I had been practicing the "learn while you earn" school of management. We decided that the only way to get a real manager, as opposed to the dweebs from Nashville tying up my phone daily, was the scientific method—get a copy of *Billboard,* the industry's Bible, and pore through it looking for managers' names and their clients.

Danny pulled out the name Ken Kragen, a Hollywood manager with a client list that included Kenny Rogers and Lionel Richie. After much discussion with Nick Hunter, a vice president at Warner Bros. and an early supporter, we all decided that Kragen would be perfect.

Following along the lines of our organized, scientific search, Nick Hunter decided on a subtle plan for contacting Kragen and convincing him to manage me—he called him on the phone and asked.

"I'm not interested in taking an entry-level act at this time," Kragen told Nick. "It's been twenty years since I've taken a new act. I'm not even sure I could do it."

Nick convinced Kragen to listen to a copy of the "Country Club" tape, then watch the video. It was the video that put it over the top. The women in Kragen's office—including Ken's wife, Kathy—said if he didn't sign me, they'd kill him.

Ken signed me without ever hearing me perform live, but he quickly rectified that with a trip to Georgia and Miss Kitty's. Luckily he liked what he saw.

And I liked what I saw, too. Ken and Danny, working from opposite ends of the record label, were quickly able to leverage my singles deal into a full album contract!

So with a hit single on the radio, climbing up the charts, doing well; packed clubs and tremendous response; great band, everything's tight, I figure I'm set. We were ready to find a top booking agency—critical for lining up the kind of dates we needed to play.

The first guy from a major booking agency, Monterey, watches the show, sees the crowd reaction, then shrugs.

"What are we supposed to do with this guy?" he says. "We don't know Travis." We finally found some bookers, Steve Lassiter and Jeffrey Beales and the William Morris Agency, to take a chance on that "dead" art form.

Okay, one hurdle cleared. Once I got over that one, there was a whopper ahead of me. If I was going to go out and tour outside my backyard, we were going to need something other than a pickup truck, a U-Haul trailer, and that one-man sound system I had scrimped for. In fact, we were starting to talk some bucks.

I started getting this creepy feeling. What if I had a hit record and went broke? I mean, what if I went from just plain dirt poor to seriously, honest-to-God broke?

I just didn't have the money to buy enough equipment to tour.

Did somebody say "tour support"?

I'd heard that phrase, "tour support," from the record company, so I figured that was surely what I needed. I went to Warner Bros. and explained my situation. They listened patiently and nodded their heads in all the right places. I paused for comment.

"Travis," the guy said, "we're not in the touring business, we're in the record business."

One more wall.

Everywhere you turn, one more wall.

All I needed was buses, sound equipment, and lights, and I had no money. Call it a challenge. Fortunately I had a manager who believed in me enough to co-sign a $100,000 loan with me.

So I had a hit record, and I went from being poor but at least owning my pickup truck to being $100,000 in the hole. God, I love show business!

And we got our first booking with the new equipment. I've still got the contract hanging on the wall in my office. A place called Zeds, right outside of Washington. A little ole tiny club that held, standing and sitting, maybe 200 people. Got paid $500 for that gig.

Welcome to the big time.

That's when I started realizing that you can't get rich off of this thing right off the bat.

Prior to my first hit record, everything I had was paid for. All my equipment was paid for, and my overhead was virtually nothing. My truck was paid for. All of a sudden, not only is it your life, but you've got the responsibility of the other guys that work in the band.

You're a corporation at that point. You're the CEO of Travis Tritt Enterprises, of which the major, sole, and only product is Travis Tritt.

Chapter 18

✿ ✿ ✿ ✿ ✿ ✿ ✿

Mr. Promotion Man

I don't care much for morning. Dawn has got to be one of the most overrated things around, if you're looking at the beginning of the day instead of the end.

But it was every morning, before dawn, load in the car and head for the first radio station.

"Hey, man. Great to meet you. My name is Travis Tritt, and I'd like for you to hear my new Warner Brothers record."

Keep smiling, like a beauty queen with Vaseline on her teeth.

"Well, yes, it is a little different from a lot of what you're playing . . ."

Ten days at a time, thirty or so radio stations at a shot. It averages out to about three radio stations a day. I started thinking of the whole promotional tour as a car rally, where we'd drive like crazy to get to a certain place at a certain time, smile like a demented person for forty-five minutes, then load back into the car and head to the next checkpoint.

"You know, Southern music's always been an important part of country music . . ."

You drove to them all, because who could afford the plane fare? You cover one region at a time. You do ten days in the Southeast—one in the morning; drive 200 miles; one in the afternoon; drive 200 miles, a third in the evening; go to sleep. Once you're done in the Southeast, you get on a plane and fly out West, or whatever, and you start all over again.

"You know, I appreciate your saying that, really. I'm sorry you don't think I'm going to make it in country music, but, you know, I'll bet I prove you wrong . . ."

Most of the time, it was strictly meet-and-greet. Watch the video, listen to the single, sign an 8×10 in case I did become famous, and schmooze a little. Most deejays are pretty good guys and gals. They like the music and are more than a little starstruck. I figured two, three at the most, would tell me that Hell would freeze over deep enough to go ice skating on before they played one of my records on their radio station, and that estimate held. A larger number would promise me they'd play my version of the telephone book if I'd send them the tape.

What bothered me was the sheer bogus-ness of it

all. I like deejays, but I'd like to do more than shake their hand and sign the picture. Maybe talk to them for more than a few seconds. The more you look at the cogs and gears behind the star-making machinery, the more uneasy you feel.

Me with Peter Frampton. *(Photo by Beth Gwinn.)*

Chapter 19

❀ ❀ ❀ ❀ ❀ ❀ ❀

Serious Road

When I finally realized that I had to make things happen myself, I started at the bottom of a very steep learning curve. It's not enough to be a singer, a song-writer, the CEO of T.T.E., I had to be a *working* CEO.

It was—and still is—a learning process. You find out what works, what you can say, and what you can't say. You learn real quick that you get more freedom and more ability to work on your own terms as your success grows. Your clout grows.

Look at the comparison between Randy Travis and Dwight Yoakam. Randy Travis was the Garth Brooks of that particular time period, 1988–89, and he was the guy, the head honcho. Mr. Nice Guy. On the other hand, I saw all the problems that somebody like

Dwight Yoakam was having. "I'm gonna do this my way. I'm gonna do it like I want to do it. If you don't like it, then kiss my ass and get out of the way."

I saw all of these things and I thought, "Where's the balance?" I wanted to take my own shots. If I didn't know the answer to something, I was at least smart enough to surround myself with people who did have a pretty good clue as to what was going on.

In 1991, after three number-one records and an album approaching platinum, I actually made some money. I got a big royalty check that wasn't committed to the bus, the sound, the lights, the band's salary, the million and one things that suck up money. I did the only intelligent thing I could do with the money. I went out and bought a new Harley.

Most people don't really grasp how really expensive it is to run a tour.

It takes literally barrels of money a day to keep a tour on the road. Buses, salaries, insurance, manager's fees, booking agent fees, all those things that come out of your pocket. Videos—guess who pays for those? They charge them right back to your account at the record company. Three hundred, four hundred thousand dollars, money that a couple of years ago would have been my definition of rich, gone in three or four months. And you don't know where it went. You're just trying to keep the show going.

Like any other business, too, there are times you invest in yourself and invest in your company. And it's not necessarily when things are going great.

A lot of artists don't understand that—there is a gamble. If you want to go out and make the impression you want to make, you're going to have to be willing to invest in yourself. I saw all this money coming in, and I hadn't had money for so long that I just wanted to put that money in my pocket. I wanted to see what it was like to live on the wealthier side of life.

Ken Kragen told me about an early Kenny Rogers booking in Vegas. Rogers and Olivia Newton-John were at the Riviera in Las Vegas. They were taking in $75,000 a week for an eight-week run. At Kragen's suggestion, instead of putting that $600,000 in their pockets, they took the whole amount and bought billboards on the sides of buses and newspaper advertisements announcing sellouts—all things that cost a lot of money. All the money he made for the week was gone, but there was a flood of people every night, lined up to get in.

By the end of the week, every show was sold out. The Riviera tore up his contract and came back with a new one—twelve weeks at $135,000 a week—a million-dollar difference. It takes guts to step out there with that investment and be willing to give up everything you just earned. What if I didn't have success? Everything I'd made was all going to be gone, and I wouldn't have anything to show for it.

It takes a lot of discipline, a lot more than people think.

For the first couple of years after "Country Club," we were touring 280 days a year. That means staying out for forty-five days at a time, doing a show every single night. Traveling 500, 600, even 800 miles between shows, overnight bus rides every night. We started talking about the Tour from Hell. After about three months, we even stopped asking where we were. There was the road, the road, and the road, a single, endless ribbon that defined our days and nights.

Sometimes we'd get a break for a personal appearance. Sometimes we'd perform. We "meeted and greeted" until we couldn't shake another hand. We were interviewed by everyone who could hold a tape recorder. And we had just enough time to have no private life.

None whatsoever.

And for me, to be able to have people consistently come up to me and say, "You know, you're really a pretty nice guy," for me to be able to do that, I have to have time away. Just for me. Time at home. Travis being Travis Tritt is a twenty-four-hour-a-day, seven-day-a-week, 365-day-a-year job. I can't go home and turn off the fact that I am a recognizable figure. I'm Travis Tritt, Country Singer. I have signed autographs at the grocery store in the middle of the night. It goes with the territory.

So what I have to do for my own sanity is have points in time when I'm able to just go away from all of this and go home. I get on a tractor. I don't go to the grocery store. I don't go to clubs. I don't go out and do a thing. I get on my farm, away from everybody, and just be me.

And a little bit of that goes a very, very long way. If I get five days at home, I can go back out for thirty days and be as nice to people as I want to be. Being on the road means getting pulled in fifty different directions at once by everybody. Everybody wants a little piece of you. You have to have a lot of patience to be able to deal with that. And if you're stressed out from doing it too long, you find yourself ripping people new assholes.

At the end of the "Country Club" Tour from Hell, I found myself after four number-one-singles, a platinum album, and a new album headed for double platinum, in the middle of a cow pasture, on a flatbed truck, with a blue light, a red light, and a white light, a sound system that might charitably be described as primitive, backing up a rodeo in the middle of Faith, South Dakota.

And I thought, "This is not helping my career at all." It's time to put the brakes on the bus. These people are not hearing me at my best—and that's cheating fans, as far as I'm concerned.

I'm a perfectionist in a lot of ways. I don't ever want to go out and not give my absolute best.

As a new artist, I was trying to get as many people as possible to recognize me, instead of saying, "Travis who?" Actually you're trying to get as many people as you possibly can to recognize you . . . before you go crazy.

The Faith, South Dakota, show was a low point. Ain't gonna do that no more.

One bad show will follow you around like a bad smell forever.

No matter how many good ones you do, if you do a shitty show one night because you don't feel good about the situation—bad sound, bad lights, whatever—you have to live with it for the rest of your career. If I don't feel like I'm doing a good show, I know good and well there's people out there in the audience who feel the same way. And I don't want them to walk away with that kind of impression.

I want, "Wow!"

Me with Otis. *(Photo by Henry Diltz.)*

Chapter 20

❀ ❀ ❀ ❀ ❀ ❀ ❀

The Mother Church

I was the youngest member inducted into the Grand
Ole Opry, and that made me proud. Partially because
the Opry is something solid, a tangible reminder of
country music's roots. At the center stage of the Opry
House there's a circle of wood floor cut from the
center stage of the old Ryman Auditorium in downtown Nashville. Hank Williams, Roy Acuff, Ernest
Tubb, Red Foley—all the greats walked across those
old planks. And the first time I walked out there, I
had this gut feeling that no matter how big country
music got, there was always an invisible cord tying it
back to this circle.

Frankly, I didn't think the Opry would ask me to
become a member. I made no secret about the fact

that I wanted to be a member, and I saw a lot of my peers, like Randy Travis and Clint Black, joining the Opry. But the Opry has never liked to extend a hand to people it perceives as outsiders.

Whenever I was offered a guest appearance and I could juggle my schedule, I always took it. Even in the new Opry House, which is more like a Las Vegas showroom than the sweaty, old Ryman, the Opry is a time machine. I could walk out on that stage, walk past Minnie Pearl, and imagine how the music must have been not all that long ago. God, it must have been simpler! Not easier, but simpler, without the sound and lights, the multiple buses and eighteen-wheelers. But whenever I walk out there and see that circle of old wood, I also think of ole Hank and the price he paid, dead by pills and liquor, only a year younger than me.

First time I played the Opry, I got this bright idea that I could play Charlie Daniels's Volunteer Jam across town the same night. No problem—I'd play the Jam in the afternoon, cruise on over to the Opry for an early-evening performance, then beat it back to the Jam for the all-star finale, with everyone from Charlie to Ted Nugent and B. B. King.

Going back and forth was like commuting between two different cultures. At the Jam, the rowdier the show, the better. At the Opry, tone it down for the older audience. Then back to the Jam.

Amazingly, it worked like clockwork. I smoked through my set at the Jam and got to the Opry in plenty of time for my two-song guest appearance. I did "Here's a Quarter" and a ballad, and was getting ready to head offstage when Jack Greene, who was hosting that night, motioned me to stay.

"Travis," he said, applauding. "Why don't you stay with us and do 'Country Club'?"

Let me explain something here. When you guest the Opry, you play two—count 'em, two—songs. If you get a spectacular reaction, it's acceptable to play the last verse of the song over again. But a third song?

Unprepared for, too!

I looked over at the band—my fiddle player kicks "Country Club" off, and he didn't have his fiddle. I signaled the guitar player to go for it, man, and we played like crazy. The crowd loved it. So I kept coming back, and every time we kept getting great responses. Finally Hal Durham, the manager of the Opry, called and asked me to join. I was thrilled, just absolutely thrilled.

I admire the Opry for its traditions, all the greats who stood on those old planks of wood.

My mother, father, aunt, and uncle went to see the Opry at the old Ryman when my mother was pregnant with me. It was one of the last performances of Patsy Cline and Hawkshaw Hawkins. They didn't drive all the way up there from Marietta, Georgia, to Nashville, Tennessee, to see a tourist attraction. They went there because the Opry was the center of the country music universe. Careers were made or broken on the stage of the Ryman. Anyone who was anyone or who aspired to be anyone played there.

You could drive up to the Opry on any given night and see Patsy Cline, Lester Flatt and Earl Skruggs, Hawkshaw Hawkins, Lonzo and Oscar, Homer and Jethro, Minnie Pearl—all the people who were legends at the time. They were the driving force in country music at that time, the hot stars. For a while it looked like the Opry was going to become more of a piece of Americana, a place for tourists rather than people looking for great music. But I think it's still important. I think it's important to reaffirm those ties with the past. We didn't just drop into country music because it was hot, planning to make our bucks and get out. We are a continuing part of the tradition, and I think we have a responsibility to understand those traditions.

That's why it really excited me to see the Opry start bringing in a lot of the new people, and the new people wanting to sign up. I love that part of it, because that insures it will go on for the future. The Opry was one of the biggest honors I've ever accepted in my life. I guess there have been three high points in my career, period. The night I joined the Opry, the day I got my first platinum record, and the day I got the Horizon award.

It took "Country Club" a year and a half to go platinum. As a matter of fact, when "It's All About the Change" was released and went gold quickly, "Country Club" was just going platinum. So Warner Bros. had a gold and platinum party for me in Nashville. The Horizon award, from the Country Music Association, was someting I had set my sights on from the very beginning. The award is, essentially, for the best up-and-coming artist of the year. The year before I won, Garth Brooks had been the winner. Other noted recipients included Randy Travis, Ricky Van Shelton, and Clint Black.

When Danny Davenport first took my first tapes to Warner Bros. in California and then on to Nashville, he had done up a professional-looking portfolio, with my background, biography, how we recorded that first album, all those things. At the very end of the presentation, he wrote, "I will make a prediction that Travis Tritt is as strong a potential winner of the Horizon award as anyone out there for the 1990 season." He missed it by one year; I got the award in 1991.

That was my first award. For the first time, I felt a part of the Nashville community. When that award came down, it said to all the naysayers, take me seriously.

Jerry Glanville, Governor Zell Miller, Waylon Jennings, and me.
(Photo by Rick Diamond.)

Chapter 21

Merle

As you cross the Mississippi in about the middle of the country, the highway begins to flatten out, a long, straight unraveling roll of Christmas ribbon, heading for the wall of the Rockies.

Open up the bus windows and look around, nine or ten o'clock in the morning, and what you see is sunlight on corn. Corn. Maybe a patch of trees here or there, willows lining a stream bed, but mostly corn, and mostly flat. Hang a left in Kansas and follow the flat down to Oklahoma, where the corn gives way to big ranches and the occasional oil derrick; dusty pickup trucks loaded with hay and wind, wind, wind. This is Western Swing country, folks weaned on Bob Wills and fiddle swing music, Saturday night at the ballroom, denims with sharp creases and Sunday-go-to-meeting hats, gingham dresses and lemonade. At least, that's how I hear it used to be, swing your partner and all. What it is now is rodeo country, and I can understand that.

Do your first rodeo, especially if you're a Southern boy like me, and you're all caught up in the pageantry. People carrying flags, cowboys, barrel racers, bull riders, all sort of like waking up in the middle of a Western movie. What rodeo means for a traveling singer is steady money, three or four days in a row, two or three shows a day. And crowds that'll go crazy for you, if you can catch their hearts. I guess it's a cliché to say that bull riders don't much keen to bullshit, but it's still true.

There were three of us in the show—bringing up the rear, me, the so-far One-Hit Wonder; Tanya Tucker, who could bring a rodeo crowd screaming to their feet without even working up a sweat; and Merle Haggard. *The* Merle Haggard. The Hag. The man who did his time standing up and then wrote "Mama Tried." A visible connection between the way country music was (the dance halls, the gingham) and the way it is (the bull riders, the hard-eyed cowgirls).

It's hard to explain my feelings about Haggard. We'd played together once before, and the easy thing is to say I was honored—no, make that awed—to stand on the same stage with him. He still carried the remnants of Bob Wills's old band, the Texas Playboys, still honed to the double-fiddle sound. He'd written songs that I'd listen to, played, *believed in,* my whole life. He was one of the pillars of the country music world I grew up in, one of its creators. Looking at him, I could see the past, the dust of California and

Oklahoma, the glitter of Music City. The first time he'd seen Johnny Cash perform, he was a prisoner in Folsom. Haggard had gone on to be not only the biggest, but the best.

But I couldn't help but have a little shudder. Looking at the Hag out there on that rodeo stage, where he'd stood a few thousand times before, I could see not only the past, but a vision of my future.

I had thirty minutes, just enough time to tickle that audience before Tanya sashayed out on stage and knocked 'em dead. But a rodeo audience is a country audience, and I damn sure knew how to play to a country audience. I rocked as hard as I knew how— slipped them a little Bob Seger, a little George Jones, the bull riders digging Seger, their parents Jones. Then I'd close with "Country Club." "I'd like to thank you all for making this our first top ten record," and meaning it every single time. Then I'd take the applause and turn it over to Tanya, who was born for that stage. That would give me time to get back to the bus, shuck the by-now stinking, sweaty leather, and get some kind of shower before Haggard's set.

I'd head back to the stage and just stand in the wings, watching Hag play, watching him effortlessly work that audience until he had them eating out of his hand. You'd look out there and see them singing along with every song, the kids and the older people alike, the songs pretty much a part of the fabric of life on the prairie for two generations. Those people didn't just "like" Haggard's music—they loved the man. They loved the music because it was a part of the man, and the man was one of them. There had been nights for them all when the bottle let them down, times when they'd chased each other 'round the floor. They knew about hungry eyes and what it was like to be on the run—from the law, the bills, the husband, the wife, the past. I had never seen a stronger bond between the man on stage and the people who paid good money to sit there and sing along.

I was there every set, and one night he motioned me out, covering the mike with his hand.

"Getting ready to sing 'Okie From Muskogee,' " he said. "If you know the words, you're welcome to join me."

If I knew the words . . . Find me ten people in country music who *don't* know the words. Heck, the chorus is probably one of the most recognizable sets of lyrics in the history of country:

> *Yes, I'm proud to be an Okie from Muskogee,*
> *A place where even squares can have a ball.*
> *We still wave Old Glory down at the courthouse*
> *And white lightning's still the biggest thrill of all.*

Everybody sang, and as we were heading offstage, Haggard said, "If you've got nothing else to do, I'd like for you to come back to the bus with me for a while."

Guess what I did?

"So play me something," Haggard said, handing me his acoustic guitar.

I thought for a moment, then began a ballad I hadn't recorded, about my father and growing up in a South that was changing. I finished and handed the guitar back to Haggard.

"You only sing from the heart, don't you?" he said.

"I try to, best I can."

"Yeah, so do I." He tuned the guitar for a second, then launched into "Mama Tried." When he finished, he handed the guitar back to me. I played "It's All About to Change," a new song. Handed the guitar back, and he played "Tonight, The Bottle Let Me Down." Handed the guitar back to me.

I suspected my list of songs would run out a bit sooner than the Hag's, but, hell, I was game. I'd play the songs I'd written, then hand the guitar back to this country legend, and he'd play me a song that was part of my life. Finally I just handed the guitar back and told him to keep the darn thing, but would he mind playing "I Am a Lonesome Fugitive"? I just kept making requests, and he just kept playing. When he stopped, most of the night seemed to have passed. Pretty soon, the sun would be creeping up over the stockyards, the cowboys getting up and stretching what could still be stretched, rubbing liniment on what couldn't, getting ready for another ride.

"Thing is," Haggard says, answering a question I hadn't had nerve enough to ask, "it's not just me out on the road. There's people who depend on me for a living. My band. If I went off the road, it'd be pretty hard on them."

So you keep playing, I say.

"I keep playing," he says. "It's what I do."

I get up and thank the man, then head back to my bus. I'll sleep until noon, and by the time I wake up, we'll be able to see the Rockies.

Marty Stuart and I rehearsing for the Grammy Awards show.
(Photo by Jim McHugh. Used with permission from the National Academy
of Recording Arts and Sciences, Inc.)

Chapter 22

❊ ❊ ❊ ❊ ❊ ❊ ❊

Bright Lights, Little City

*Y*ou could see the lights of Vegas from a long, long way away.

"Country Club" was moving up the charts. The album was in the works, and we had a booking in Vegas—with Charlie Daniels, no less.

I sat up on the bus as we were coming into town around 5 a.m. The rest of the band was sleeping, and the whole scene reminded me of an old Kristofferson song, the one where he sings that if you ain't bombed in Birmingham, then you ain't one of us. Band's sleeping, and I'm stuck inside a song. Vegas had got me thinking of that old youth pastor years before, and I was wondering if he and his chosen were still in Vegas.

The song I was writing was "Bible Belt," and I was caught up in the song.

And that's how I felt, disconnected from the "real" world, optimistic, worried, tired, when we crossed the dam a mile outside of town and the lights of the Strip tinged the horizon.

"C'mon guys! Everybody up!" I went the whole length of the bus, rousting everybody. "You gotta see this!"

So we all stood there, everybody rubbing the sleep out of their eyes, looking at the lights of Vegas coming up on the road in front of us. It wasn't spoken, but we were all thinking, "All right! Made it."

We sat and watched as the bus rolled into the town that never sleeps. When we got to the hotel where we were playing, there was a huge sign, a spectacular sign, a sign just about the size of the biggest building in Marietta. It read: "Tonight! The Charlie Daniels Band! Two Shows!" We stood looking at the sign for a long time, waiting, I suppose, for it to change its message.

"Do you suppose this is the right place?" someone, I don't remember who, asked.

I couldn't reach the hotel people, and when Ken Kragen finally did, they were blunt. "Travis Tritt and the Country Club Band? On the sign out front? Get real!"

Well, at least we were in Vegas. After sleeping and checking the place out, we were ready for the sound check, so we hauled our stuff to the dressing room. Only there wasn't exactly a dressing room. It was actually a closet, right behind the stage. There wasn't even a mirror on the wall; there was an old bathroom mirror leaning against the wall, propped at a precarious angle. There was a table of some sort, a small pitcher of water and a pile of Dixie cups. Backstage condiments, as it were. Over in the corner was a barrel of sweeping compound, although the hotel had the grace to remove the broom. There were no hooks on the walls, no place to hang anything. Just throw your clothes on the floor, boys, and let's rock!

We looked like a bunch of rubes who just discovered there was no Easter Bunny when we turned around and practically ran into the huge, hulking form of Charlie Daniels. I knew about Charlie Daniels, but I'd never met him until that moment. I'd always thought he was cool, because he'd done one of the best shows I'd ever seen, on his Full Moon tour in Atlanta.

Charles Daniels was a big operation. He was one of the few people on the road who had eight buses and ten tractor-trailers, and every year they would paint the trucks with the new album cover. Way cool. I saw him at the Fox Theater in Atlanta, and, man, that was one of the best, tightest shows I've ever been to in my life. He brought out cloggers and dancers, played country and rock, didn't pay the slightest attention to any artificial musical boundaries. I'd learned a lot about performing, about working an audience, just from standing there watching Charlie Daniels. Discovering his music came at a very important time in my life, and I was a huge admirer.

He stuck out a hand the size of a slab of ham and shook. Then he looked around. And started getting red in the face, like an impending thunderstorm. Or maybe an earthquake.

"You boys pick up your stuff and come with me," he said, heading out toward his own dressing room.

We followed along like baby ducks behind our mommy. He led us to a huge room, with wall-to-wall mirrors, bright lights and a huge pile of food and drink.

"You guys use my dressing room from now on," he said, introducing us to his band. "Anybody has any question with that, tell 'em to talk to Charlie."

He watched our show almost every night, and just before we packed it in, he took me aside in one of the stairwells.

"I think you're gonna be in this business a long time," he said. "Just remember one thing—keep finding out what your audience wants, and give it to them, every time."

I nodded. It seemed like such simple advice, but I'd already started getting a hint of just how hard it would be.

Charlie's seen the rock 'n' roll side and the country side, from both ends of the spectrum. That's why I like to take to heart the things Charlie has said to me, the things George Jones has said to me, the things Johnny Cash has said to me, the things Waylon Jennings has said to me. Pats on the back from those guys mean a whole lot, because those are guys who have really been there. If they see something in me that they dig, then hopefully I'll be around a while, too.

Charlie's audience was good. Rodeo people—not your typical Vegas crowd. Most of the Vegas people go see a show and don't really know who they're going to see. They see a big name on the billboard, Reba McIntyre, and it's, "Oh yeah, I saw her on a Bob Hope special once." They don't have any idea what her music is. They're just in town, and when you're in Vegas, you go to see famous people.

It's either go see George Strait down the street, or walk across town to see Dionne Warwick over at another place, or we'll go right down the street here . . .

Second trip to Vegas: Barbara Mandrell was the headliner and, in huge letters on the sign, "Travis Tritt."

I told the guys, again, that we had *really* arrived. I was thrilled. Here we are, we've got our name on the billboard, we're up there. And every night we sold out the shows. Lines that would go all the way out the doors, past the casino, out through the building and down the street. That kind of crowd every night, two shows a night.

The second night, in between the first show and the second show, I went back to my room to change clothes. The only way to go was to go back through the casino, so I walked past the whole line and not one single person recognized me—little twinge, there.

I was getting ready to get on the elevator, and there was an older lady standing there talking to her husband. She said, "Well, what time does that nice Randy Travis start playing?"

I got a lot of mileage out of that story. There's certain acts that can play Vegas and can get away with it. Maybe I'm one of those who can't.

Dad and me on our first great motorcycle trip together.
(Photo by Jackie Williams.)

Chapter 23

✦ ✦ ✦ ✦ ✦ ✦

The Album Puzzle

When you sit down to do an album, every song has a purpose.

That doesn't mean every song has to have a deep meaning or great social impact. A song can be just plain fun. But creating an album is like putting together a jigsaw puzzle when you're not sure just what the picture actually is. The songs are the building blocks of the album. For a few minutes, divorce yourself from the content of the songs and think about their structure. There are ballads, up-tempo songs, flat-out rockers, ones that fall between categories. There are songs that work better "unplugged," with a minimum of instrumentation, songs that will only work with an Allman Brothers–style double guitar, double drum-set band, and songs that need a touch of "sweetening," adding a bit of this and that. Content-wise, there are cry-in-your-beer ballads, lost loves and bitter statements, a funny pun, a cowboy story, songs I wrote, songs from other songwriters . . . the list goes on and on.

So what you have to do is sit down with your producer and listen to hundreds of tapes, then try to imagine how each of those songs would fit into the evolving whole of the album.

Find out what your audience wants, and give it to them every time . . .

Charlie Daniels's words are always there when I start putting together an album. I have this great labo-ratory for finding out what my audience wants—it's called The Road. In the course of 100 shows, I can stick a song into the lineup and see how the audience responds. One night might not tell me anything—there are nights when you could sing the lyrics from a telephone book and have the crowd go wild, and there are nights when, well, the opposite happens. But, taken on an average, I can get a feeling for a song.

A good song is the basic building block of an album. I define a good song as one that will stand the test of time.

Good songs can stand any treatment. Look how many good songs have been cut over and over again by numerous artists and go to the top of the charts. Dolly Parton's "I Will Always Love You," just for instance. It's been a huge country hit *and* one of the biggest hits in the history of rock—because it's a good song. It can stand any artist's treatment.

Or Willie Nelson's songs.

They just keep coming back. They're direct; they're straightforward, and you don't have to be a literature major to understand them. They're songs for now, and they're songs for twenty years from now. They stand the test of time.

That's the thing that I try to look for. Is this going to be a song that somebody who's cruising down the road in their truck is going to say, "Well, that's a catchy little tune," then turn the radio off, get out of the truck, and forget about it? Or is the song going to register, to ring some bell deep in their head? "Oh my God, that's exactly what I've been trying to say!"

Makes it hard to put together an album.

The way I think about an album, I don't much believe in "filler" material. I've always had the opinion that if you have seven singles on the album and you only get to release five—five is the standard number of single releases per album—that's a good problem to have. You hope you have that problem on every album, and so far I have been fortunate.

There are always going to be certain songs that are referred to as "career songs," songs that push your career to a whole new level. For me, the song was "Here's a Quarter, Call Someone Who Cares." You don't have career songs on every album. Wish that was possible—it probably is, if you're Merle Haggard. If you start thinking you can have a career song on each and every album, you're going to be very disappointed very quickly. It's like stepping up to the plate believing that at least once every game you're going to slam one out of the park with the bases loaded. Maybe the same batter has the same potential every night, but every night it's a different world, a different game. Synchronicity—the bat's right, the pitch is perfect, the wind is blowing the right way, you just feel stong—wham, it's gone. The next night, you may feel every bit as strong, but, wham, it's a base hit.

I mention this because, as a songwriter, there's a temptation to sit down and say I feel strong, let's go for the long ball. Here comes another "Quarter." It doesn't work. I wish it did. Instead, your focus has to be on good songs. If I write a good song, a song that resonates with me and hopefully with you, the long balls will take care of themselves.

Picking songs for an album is all about educated guesses; at least, that's what I try to do. Test them out before I decide to release them.

I played "Quarter" on stage for a year and a half before I recorded it, and every night it was phenomenal. I knew that song had to be on the next album. I had executives explain to me that it was a "novelty" song, and everybody in Nashville knew that novelty songs never went anywhere. Call it what you want, I said. Put it in any category you want to put it in, but the fact of the matter was that the song clicked with the audience and was going on the album.

Realistically, though, it comes down to this: You throw it out there, and you hope it's going to do well. You can test it, you can research it, you can do what you want to; you can have an educated guess and think that this is gonna be a good thing, and go with your instincts, but nobody—that's nobody, not record companies, radio people, artists, writers—knows if the song is going to be the smash you might think it could or should be.

Everybody I've ever met in Nashville knows the secret of hit records. A million people, and every one of them has a formula for picking a hit single. They're all wrong. If they weren't, there'd be just this one big mansion on the hill, and a big line standing outside, waiting to get The Word.

When I first came to Nashville and first started talking to record people, they told me, "You've got the basic ideas, but we need to connect you to some experienced songwriters."

"Why?" I asked.

"A radio hit has to have the hook within the first thirty seconds of the song," I was told. "All professional songwriters know that. The song can't be over three and a half minutes long, has to have some catch phrase that is instantly recognizable, has to rhyme. Things like that."

"Of course," I replied.

Maybe there's software or something: How to Write a Hit Song, Version 1.0.

"By the way," I was told as an afterthought. "Don't do anything acoustic, because it's way too controversial for drive-time radio."

Hear that, Randy Travis? Guess your song "Promises," a big hit, will have to go.

There is no specific formula.

The only thing that creates a hit is whether or not it clicks with the audience. And you never know that till you get done.

Truth be told, I fought the release of "Country Club" as my first single. I didn't write the song; to me it didn't seem to fit into my format. I wouldn't have written a song like that. Guess this means that I don't have the big secret either. But "Country Club" taught me a big lesson—it changed the way I listened to a song. I had been on the road too much, spent too much time in those sleazy little clubs, and I'd gotten away from listening to my own music as a fan does. I picked the next single, "Help Me Hold On," and it went to number one. I went to the record company and struck a deal—I get to pick the singles, until I pick the wrong one. I have made a couple of questionable calls since, but they still give me the last word.

A record doesn't have to be a chart hit to be a success. "Put Some Drive in Your Country" was the lowest-charted record I have ever had, but it established my style and sold a ton of albums. "Can I Trust You with My Heart" was number one for two weeks on every single chart—*Billboard, Radio & Records, Cashbox*—for two weeks, but my album sales jumped more for the release of "T-R-O-U-B-L-E," which died at number eleven.

Everybody out there is a music critic. And, just like the formula for what is a hit and what's not a hit, everyone is all wrong once in a while. Most radio stations have a formula, and either the song fits their formula or it doesn't. Radio programmers pay a fortune to researchers and consultants to tell them what their market wants to hear. This song is too "rock" ("T-R-O-U-B-L-E," for instance), too country, too this or too that.

When "Country Club" was released, I was going around playing concert dates and trying to get things off the ground. I went to a station in Baltimore and really pitched the program director hard.

"Why," I asked, "are you not playing 'Country Club'?"

"Too 'bubba' for our format," the program director, Bob Moody, told me. "Our audience, according to the research we have, doesn't drive pickup trucks. Our audience is more into the Reba McIntyre, refined sort of country music. This is an area where country is just starting to break out, and 'bubba' doesn't fit our format."

I accepted that, and I walked out of the station. Like most stations, they had a stack of copies of their current play list on the receptionist's desk, so I grabbed one. I noticed that Charlie Daniels's "Simple Man," as "bubba" a song as ever existed, was number thirteen on the list. On the way back to the motel, right in the heart of rush-hour drive-time, they played Hank, Jr.'s "Dixie on My Mind," which happens to be nothing short of the "bubba" national anthem.

At dinner that night with Moody, I just couldn't resist it.

"Let me just ask you a question," I said. "On the way back to the hotel, I saw about six pickups with your bumper sticker on them. You've got 'Simple Man' as number thirteen, and that's about taking drug doers out in the swamp, tying them up, and feeding them to the alligators. You're playing 'Dixie on My Mind' at drive-time. Can you fill me in on that?"

He gave me some mumbo jumbo. A week later, I got a call at home from a record exec, Bill Mayne from Warner Bros. He'd had a conversation with Bob Moody I might be interested in.

"I've been thinking an awful lot about what Travis said the other night," Moody told Mayne. "You know what? He's absolutely right."

"Good," Mayne said. "So you're going to play 'Country Club'?"

"No," he replied. "We're going to drop 'Simple Man.' "

I was on tour with Charlie Daniels at the time, and I had to go back and tell Charlie Daniels how I got his record dropped off a major radio station.

Hell, I was born to be in promotions!

It's a game that you can't understand—and if you try to figure it out you're just wasting your time. Everybody's got their own opinion and everybody is not going to like everything. There is no set, programmed way to say, "This is what our format is and we don't go outside those boundaries." You can't have a blanket policy and make it work.

How many times have you heard a record on the radio for the first time, and you might know who the artist is, you might not. The first time you hear it, you think what a piece of crap it is. Four or five days later, you hear it again, and before you know it your whole attitude about the song has changed. You feel completely different about it. That's why radio stations shouldn't have a blanket format. You might hate a song one day and like it the next.

"Based on our research"—I've always liked that one. Kind of makes you think of rocket science. I think it was Duke Ellington who said there are two kinds of music, good and bad, and that's it. All these barriers have been put up over the years because of chasing the almighty dollar. But from a songwriter's standpoint, if you sit down to write "commercial," you're dead before you ever start.

Chapter 24

❀ ❀ ❀ ❀ ❀ ❀ ❀

American Eagles and Me

My dad started riding motorcycles when I was a kid. He had a couple of Hondas and rode those for years, but he finally bought his first Harley when I was in junior high school. It was loaded, one of those motorcycles you look at and try to figure out whether it's got air-conditioning, too.

I knew that was what I wanted.

I wanted a Harley Davidson, top of the line, with everything on it. I kept telling myself, forget Vegas, I'd know I'd made it when I could cruise down to the Harley dealership in Atlanta—that's where my dad got his bikes—and pay cash for that Harley.

And that's what I finally got to do. I bought that bike, brand-new, with everything on it you can get on it. It felt great. The greatest feeling in the world. I went down to Atlanta to get the bike, had my dad take me down, since I was going to ride it back. Of course, I hadn't ridden that much. The only motorcycle I'd ever owned was an old Yamaha I had while I was married, and I hadn't even been on a motorcycle in almost two years. No problem. Travis Tritt, Country Star, can surely ride a hog.

The driveway coming out of the Harley dealership was very steep, right down to the main expressway, with a little office building across the street. I figured I'd cross the street and get comfortable with it before taking it home. I got down to the bottom of the hill, put my foot down to balance, and almost dropped the brand-new thing on the ground. Right off the bat. Scared me so bad I went to my dad and said, "You ride it home." Travis Tritt, Country Star, proving that discretion was indeed the better part of valor.

But it was a great feeling, just watching my dad ride it home. That Harley was the first thing I had to show for all those years of working. And it also was something to show my dad, too, after all those years of naysaying. You're riding what country music did for me, $13,000 worth of new, black Harley, cash on the barrel head.

I've still got the bike, plus two others. One, a beautiful Heritage Nostalgia Softtail. The other is a stripped-down speed demon, a 1991 Low Rider I got to carry on the road with me, so I'll have a bike to ride.

I did the Harley Davidson television special, then the radio version of the show. They like me, and I like them. Heck, it's getting so you can't even be a country music singer without a big ole Harley. Marty

Stuart doesn't have one, but, hey, what do you expect from a guy with all those suits? Guess he's afraid the helmet would mess up his hair.

I've always been real conservative when it comes to spending money. You get a big check today doesn't mean you get a big check tomorrow. Maybe it comes from growing up and not having a whole lot; not poor, but never a lot of extravagances.

So I haven't built the castle yet.

You get a few hit records, and people expect the castle. We'll make it easy for you—sign the paper; you'll be a star forever, after all. And when money starts flowing, it pours and, in no time at all, you're cranking right up there with the big boys.

One morning you wake up and you're fifty years old, been making a mil, two mil, five mil a year for x number of years, and you find yourself booking 280 nights a year, two shows a night for "cash flow." I've sat there talking to great artists, and just shaken my head. Where did it all go? How many cars can you own? Was flying around in a Learjet really worth it?

I've always been in this thing for the long haul, and what I learned from my raising was that you can only live over your head for so long. What do I need and what do I want? What can be practical here? Am I in this for the long haul, or am I in this for bang, bang, how much money can I make now and get out?

I don't want to go back and play the little clubs again. I don't want to have to make my living where the opening act is a gunfight. I think success is measured not so much in all the material things you've obtained, but in your decision making. Being able to make a decision not because you have to for financial reasons, but because it's something you want to do.

I am not a money-driven person.

I went looking for my first house, and I said, "What are my priorities here?"

I wanted to stay in Georgia. Out of a group that includes Alan Jackson, Trisha Yearwood, Doug Stone, and T. Graham Brown, I'm the only country music artist who's from Georgia and still lives in Georgia. Because my roots are here. Reminds me of who I was when I first started. Could have gone to Nashville; could have gone to L.A. I had real estate people sending me pictures of houses in Beverly Hills that were . . . well, excessive. Could've done that, mortgaged myself to the hilt. But I decided not to. I bought seventy-five acres of farmland with a four-year-old house—three bedrooms, two baths, 2,800 square feet—and that's all I need. It's perfect for me. Got a Harley Davidson pinball machine that rumbles when you play it, a gold record of Elvis's, a radio-controlled boat for my little swimming pool.

The first time I got asked to do *Lifestyles of the Rich and Famous*, I cracked up laughing and refused to do it. Check my refrigerator for Brie, and see if you can get those Playmates out of the pool.

I still have the first pickup truck that I ever bought in 1981, when I graduated from high school. That was my only vehicle, along with the bikes—until recently, when I went crazy and bought another pickup truck.

This business can change awfully fast. Look at the "old" days, twenty years ago. An artist like Terry Gibb could have one great hit, "Somebody's Knockin'," and be in the business forever. One hit record, and she lived off it for years. Why? Because country fans used to remember. Bill Anderson might not have a hit for years and years, but his fans would come out for him.

One thing that has always struck me is the bond between country music singers and their audiences. It was not a total singer-fan type relationshp. It was more like family. The fans saw a country music singer as a member of the family who made good, and they were honored to have that member of the family back into their homes.

But with the huge success of country in recent years has come a major change. It's more like pop music now—we're shrinking down to Andy Warhol's fifteen minutes of fame. "Stars" come and go quickly.

You try to make it last as long as you can, but you can't take it for granted that every album is going to be platinum.

The "World after Garth"—it's a different world. There are more new artists. Every time I turn on the country stations, I hear four or five new artists coming on like crazy.

Some of the acts I opened for a few years ago who were monsters are out there now beating the circuit that I was playing when I started. Not because they want to, but because they have to.

I like heavyweight fighter Joe Louis's theory. Retire while you're still at your highest point. Let them remember you for your biggest moment, not for what you became. The Michael Jordan school of life. If I never have another hit record, if I bomb tomorrow, I'll sit at home, have a new truck, and fish, and I'll have everything I need to sustain me.

I don't ever want to do something because I have to do it. I'm just so damn stubborn. I'm the kind of person if I know I've got to do it, that makes it that much harder. I prefer to do something on my own initiative, even if it's the same thing. If I *have* to go out and meet with a hundred and twenty-five people before the show every night, that's a drag. If I go out there and meet those people because I *want* to do it, it changes the whole complexion. I can live with it.

I can live with me.

Chapter 25

❀ ❀ ❀ ❀ ❀ ❀ ❀

Whose Fans, Anyway?

I did a show in South Carolina, I believe it was with Lynyrd Skynyrd, Charlie Daniels, and me. When I got into town, I did what I always do—turn on the radio station to see if anyone was promoting the concert. The country music station was not saying a word about the show. I flipped over to the rock station, and they were raving about the upcoming Lynyrd Skynyrd show, with special guest Charlie Daniels.

Oh, well. We pulled the buses up to a huge outdoor venue, 15,000 people. I was peeking out the blinds, looking at hundreds of people coming in. I saw tattoos, rebel flags, Jim Beam and Jack Daniel's, and I started thinking worrisome thoughts. "They hear me do a ballad outside today, when they're all fired up for Skynyrd, they're gonna boo me off the stage.''

I just prepared for it, accepted it. Human sacrifice time. Took a deep breath, walked out on stage and did my stuff, up-tempo and ballads, just as country as you please. We got three standing ovations. That taught me you can never really pinpoint an audience—audiences are smarter than the people who want to tie them down.

Audiences are a constant learning experience. Every year in Detroit they have a huge downtown hoedown, thousands of people, as far as you can see. I walked out on stage and, without really thinking, opened with a Bob Seger tune. Call this a fortuitous accident, since Detroit was Seger's hometown. I didn't even realize what was going on. People were just going crazy. Maybe it wasn't totally for me, but I really didn't care.

Then there was the night at Billy Bob's huge honky-tonk in Texas, me and Clint Black, when they ran out of beer. World's largest honky-tonk, and they ran out of beer.

I think my favorite venue of all the venues I've played is the Fox Theater in Atlanta. I did my first major opening for anybody there, Dwight Yoakam and Buck Owens. I had just been signed to the label but didn't have the single out yet. That night was probably an indication of how humble one's beginnings can be.

We pulled up to the backstage with all these tour buses and trucks, slid my pickup truck in between the big rigs, and helped the band unload the gear. Wasn't my idea of how things were supposed to be. I also saw one of the strangest shows I'd ever seen there,

Larry Gatlin filming a television special, which was basically four and a half hours of "Larry, we didn't catch that, we gotta do this again."

Me and a couple of buddies of mine bought two pints of Jim Beam and stuck it down in our jeans and went in. We were sitting way up in the balcony, and we just sat there and drank. Before Larry came on, we got the idea that it would be fun to leave for a while, go across the street and ride the mechanical bull in the bar over there.

We all go across the street to ride the bull, the Jim Beam's gone, and we can't even read the waiver we signed. I climbed on that bull, got a good hold, and was thrown straight up toward the ceiling, which I think I hit. There were mats on the floor, but through clever twisting in the air, I was able to smack my head into the bull's fiberglass stand.

All I remember about the whole thing was when I hit, I heard everyone in the place go, "Umf!" Which was short for, "God that must've hurt," and it did. My ear bled for two days after that, and I don't think I heard a word Gatlin sang.

Hank Williams, Jr., and me. *(Photo by Rick Moxley.)*

Chapter 26

❋ ❋ ❋ ❋ ❋ ❋ ❋

Outlaws

Here's a fact for you:

Ninety pecent of the people that I've met in this business with a rep for being "hard to deal with or real assholes" turned out to be some of the nicest people I've ever met. Pretty early, I started to figure out what "hard to deal with" actually meant—people who stood up for themselves at some point. What got them the reputation was saying, "This is wrong." I guess the ideal situation is having a manager who says that for you. Randy Travis is considered to be "the nicest guy in the world," but his manager (and wife), Lib Hatcher, is considered to be "hard to deal with." But the fact is she sees to it that Randy never gets screwed in a business deal.

Unfortunately, if you're pretty much doing everything for yourself, you quickly lose the "nice guy" tag.

And, okay, I have obviously failed Subtle 101.

Someone asked me whether I liked a contemporary country song, and I said I didn't. I didn't expect to read my comments in the *National Enquirer*.

I was talking with an interviewer from Raleigh, North Carolina, and at the end of the interview the guy said to me, "I have to tell you, you're nothing like what I thought you were going to be."

"What do you mean by that?" I asked, knowing what was coming.

"Well, I just figured, given the rep you have, that you're hard to deal with—don't mess with him. He's the guy in black; he's the guy in leather; he's the outlaw, and he'd just as soon smack you in the face as look at you."

He was embarrassed.

"I mean, that's what I heard about you, you know."

Yeah, right.

I'm a songwriter. It's what I do. Comes out of being on forty acres and learning to work hard for a living. Comes out of two marriages that blew up. Loading trucks, working my way up to inside sales. Inside sales, calling people on the phone and selling them air-conditioners. People look at you, and they've got just the perfect little box for you, the perfect little category. Call you redneck. Call you hillbilly. Like those were insults; like the words tell a person everything they need to know about James Travis Tritt:

I've been called a hillbilly,
I've been called a redneck too.
But I ain't backwards, dumb or poor,
Just red, white and blue.

I hate those little boxes, little categories. I've seen them just about kill some of my good friends, strangling off their creativity until there was almost nothing left. It's happened before in Nashville; I suspect it's going to happen again. But before we go on, let me tell you about "outlaws."

I like that image, outlaw. It's an old and venerable word, one that's carved out its own niche in country music.

It started out as sort of an insider's joke, a song written by a veteran Nashville songwriter that got great response at the picking parlors and guitar pullings that drive the Nashville star-making machinery.

"Ladies," wrote Lee Clayton, "love outlaws . . . Like babies, love stray dogs . . ."

Kris Kristofferson loved it, and Waylon Jennings was just flat crazy about it. Outlaws, stray dogs, right out of the cowboy movies. So it wasn't all that much of a surprise when, around 1973 or so, a gossip columnist told a North Carolina disc jockey that this crazy music getting started in Nashville was "outlaw music."

The name stuck, and stuck with a vengeance. Within a year, country music was experiencing its first huge boom. Driven by the likes of Willie and Waylon, the music was, for the first time, drawing in the kids, the young people, the rock audience. The music was hard and driving, my kind of music, unreconstructed honky-tonk music that used to belong to the Allman Brothers, Lynyrd Skynyrd, and the Marshall Tucker Band.

Hell, call me outlaw, I'll take it.

For me, it meant one thing, doing my music my own way, which is what Waylon did and Hank, Jr., and old Hank did before him. And fighting the establishment, because there is always an establishment.

Doesn't have anything to do with being hard to deal with, being a professional hard boy. But that's the label, and labels spread very quickly. Do all the positive things in the world, and the one negative thing you do will stand out and be talked about. That's how reputations are formed.

Country music is a very conservative industry. It likes to act like it's real liberal, but realistically it's as conservative an industry as there is. Just because your executives get to come to work in cowboy boots and embroidered shirts doesn't mean that the basic philosophy underlying the business is particularly enlightened. What they want is for you to tow the line. You have a producer who knows how to do this, and somebody will be along to do your hair for you, and all you have to do is stand up there and sing.

I've always had a real hard time with that. If I'd just been a singer, maybe it would have been different. If I'd just been a songwriter, maybe it would have been different. But I was the singer, the songwriter, the booker, the manager, the everything. And I felt nobody knew my music better than I did. I knew what worked for my audience from years and years of playing those clubs and 'tonks. I found out what worked the hard way, and that was always my argument.

"Look, if you're willing to come out on the road

with me and be there every single night and watch what happens when I play this particular song, if you're willing to do that, then I'll let you pick my singles for me. But don't tell me what works and what doesn't with my audience 'cause nobody's closer to that or knows better than I do."

Hard to deal with . . .

I always managed to somehow get my way, which, like I said, builds up that reputation all the more. The industry is uncomfortable with intelligent artists. They don't like it. It's like being in the army—the less you know the easier you are to work with.

The business is so weird. I'd go to Danny Davenport's house when he was working artists like Prince, ZZ Top and Madonna and just pick his brain. What is album-oriented rock? What gets played and what doesn't? What will guarantee that you don't get played? What are the hot cities and the cold cities for radio? It was like trying to negotiate some maze. Bottom line—country is what radio thinks is country. What does radio think is country? Who knows?

Music is an *opinion*; everybody doesn't like everything. About half the people who come to Nashville only know that they want to be a star, and they're willing to hitch their wagon to anyone who can get them there. This makes for a big market in shoddy wagons.

During the filming of the video for "Put Some Drive in Your Country."
(Photo by Ken Kragen.)

Chapter 27

❋ ❋ ❋ ❋ ❋ ❋ ❋

Me and Billy Ray

I got the strangest letter from Larry Gatlin: "Travis, I've met you on several different occasions," he wrote. "I remember still the first time I met you, and you've always impressed me as being a personable down-home Southern guy. A few years ago, I took it upon myself to become the police officer of country music to determine what was good and what was bad and what should be played and what shouldn't. That period of time was one of the most miserable points I can remember in my career, because it's not my place to be the police officer of country music. I back up everything that you said. 'Achy Breaky Heart' is a piece of shit. But don't ruin yourself and ruin your attitude about the music business and life in general because of one thing you feel you need to police. Your friend, Larry Gatlin."

I don't suppose you'd buy it if I said I didn't know the gun was loaded?

I was misquoted?

Taken out of context?

Captured by aliens and forced to utter those "Achy Breaky" words?

Fan Fair—if you're ever going to be captured by aliens, this is the place it's going to happen. Millions of fans in Nashville, tramping out to the fairgrounds to get an autograph from their favorite star. All the stars have booths, and for x hours a day you sit at your booth, signing autographs like there's no tomorrow. Sometimes the line is hours and hours long. It's a great chance to get to know your fans but it does have a tendency to leave fans and artists exhausted.

When you're not in the booth, you're usually somewhere doing interviews, since there are about a billion and a half media people in town, each one with those little bitty tape recorders or a whole film crew. And your publicist, if he or she is any good, stacks up those interviews like airplanes waiting to land in Atlanta. You sit in a little room and listen to them circling outside while you answer the same question for the fiftieth time.

Interview number three had gone great. The guy from the Associated Press knew country music, was familiar with my songs, and was interesting to talk to. I was tired, a little punchy, but the interview had perked me up. I was beginning to think I might survive another Fan Fair.

"Before we get out of here," the interviewer said, "one more question."

"Sure."

"What do you think of Billy Ray Cyrus?"

I shrugged. "I haven't seen his show, so I can't say anything about that. I haven't seen the man personally, so I can't say anything about him personally. I haven't listened to his albums, so I can't make a statement about that. But I have seen the video, and I have heard 'Achy Breaky Heart,' and I don't care for either one of them."

"Why?" he asked.

I didn't have all that many strong feelings there, but I've never been one to keep my mouth shut.

"First of all, the song doesn't really make much of a statement," I said. "It just seems kind of frivolous. The video doesn't appeal to me because it shows him stepping out of a limousine in front of thousands and thousands of fans, and nobody's even heard of this guy. Garth Brooks didn't even do that. It doesn't seem very realistic to me."

And that was it, end of interview.

I walked over to my publicist, Nancy Russell, and my manager, and I said, "I just made a statement in there that may give me some flak. The reporter said his story would go out on the newswire in three weeks, so we ought to be prepared."

The next day I was headlining the Warner Brothers show. When I came back on the bus, somebody said, "Are you listening to this?"

"Listening to what?" I replied, and he turned up the radio.

It was Carl P. Mayfield, one of the afternoon guys from WSIX in Nashville, taking people's phone calls on what they thought about my comments on Billy Ray Cyrus.

159

The wire had moved the story that morning to newspapers and radio stations around the country. I believe the spin was something like "Country's bad boy slams new idol." Something like that.

"Let's open up the phone lines and see what people have to say about the Travis Tritt–Billy Ray feud."

Well, there were people who agreed with me, and there were people who disagreed.

Only sometime, over the next few days, every bad comment about Billy Ray got attributed to me. You'd think I suggested that he be hauled out and shot.

I got a call from Marty Stuart, who was cackling like an old woman. "You really did it this time, brother! You couldn't have opened a bigger can of worms if you'd said Roy Acuff was gay."

Marty and I thought it was pretty funny, except that it refused to go away. Finally, after hearing the last set of comments on Nashville radio, I called the station and said I was on the way down.

Once I got settled in the studio, I said, "Ask away."

"Did you make these statements?" one of the radio station personnel asked.

I said, "Yes, I did."

"Why?"

"I was asked an honest question, and I gave an honest answer. Nothing personal. But nobody out there in this world can say they like every song they've ever heard. Billy Ray may not like every song that I've ever done; that's okay. But I don't want to see this thing get blown out of proportion. And I don't want to see country music get to the point where it's turned into an ass-wiggling contest."

I apologized to Billy Ray, told him I hoped he sold ten million copies of the record. Went home. I sent

Billy Ray a peace lily and a get-well card because I heard he'd been feeling bad enough to cancel his Fan Fair appearance.

Headline in the local paper the next day: "Travis Tritt Trashes Billy Ray Cyrus."

The more I said about it, trying to rectify the situation, the worse it got. So I just said nothing more. Hell, I even read Marty's remark, twisted around and pointed at me, in the *Atlanta Journal-Constitution*: "Even Travis Tritt's longtime friend Marty Stuart has turned against him, by saying he couldn't have opened a bigger can of worms if he'd said Roy Acuff was gay."

If I had it to do over again, I'd do the exact same thing. Because I still defend my opinion. If this was rock and roll, nobody would even notice. If Sammy Hagar revealed he didn't really like Rod Stewart, I doubt that it would rate a headline anywhere, except maybe *MTV News*. But I broke the cardinal rule of country music, and I didn't even realize it.

You just don't say anything negative about anything, period.

We are all country buds.

I was interviewed the other day, I don't remember who it was, but the guy was talking about the philosophy of my music, that I have a different approach. I agreed and said I thought that was good.

"Well, isn't that exactly what Billy Ray Cyrus is trying to do?" he said.

"Well, I made my statements. I stand by what I said. Everything else is just media trash. Let's get on with it. Just quit beating this thing to death and move along."

And the guy said, "So, in other words, are you

saying that you're not saying anything because you don't need to anymore or because it's prudent not to?"

"I've never been prudent about anything," I said. "I say what I think; I say what's on my mind. In country, your audience wants to know more about what you are and what you're all about. What you do when you're not on stage. What the real person is like. That's what the fans want to know. And to get up there and to lie about something or to withhold feelings just because it's not prudent, I think that is wrong."

We're all people out here, trying to make a living at something that just happens to be very much in constant scrutiny. It may absolutely kill my image, but when I go home I don't get up every day and wash my hair, and blow dry it, and put on leather jeans and fringe jackets. I get up and throw on a ready pair of blue jeans and put on a baseball cap and get on my tractor and mow hay.

Waylon, one of the original outlaws, set me right.

"I've been accused of doing that very same thing, opening my mouth, for so many years," he told me. "Basically all I was doing was throwing something out there to see if the folks in Nashville had a sense of humor. I found out a long time ago that most of them don't. But I do."

Heck, if you look at the positive side, Billy Ray and I got more press and more recognition off that one statement than anything we could have tried to manufacture. As a matter of fact, my publicist at the time was accused of staging the whole thing.

I understand the system a little bit better now.

And having the label of "outlaw" is not all bad. It gives people something to talk about. You don't fall between the cracks, another "Now, who's this guy again?"

I remember being in the offices at Warner Bros. the first time that Randy Travis hit the tabloids. There were a lot of smiles. I asked why everybody was grinning.

"No matter what it is, if you're big enough to make the *National Enquirer* or the other tabloids, you know you're big," they told me, as if I was a little kid who hadn't picked up on the joke yet, "whether they say negative or positive. Because they don't print stuff about people who don't sell papers." Since then, I personally have been waiting to be linked romantically to the Space Alien.

There's a reason that the cliché "It's only rock and roll" came into being. It ain't brain surgery here. I've talked to Billy Ray Cyrus since, and no lightning bolts came down from the clouds. I hope "Old Outlaws Like Us" puts some closure on the subject, but if it doesn't, so what?

It isn't the end of the world.

Clint Black, me, and Ralph Emery on *Nashville Now.*
(Photo by Ken Kragen.)

Chapter 28

❀ ❀ ❀ ❀ ❀ ❀ ❀

The Star-Maker Machinery

I never get tired of people telling me I'm not as big of a pain-in-the-ass as they thought I was going to be.

That's a pretty big compliment when they finally come back and tell me. I've thought a lot about this whole outlaw thing. It was there in the beginning because my music has always been different from the prevailing trends of the times. It is on the edge. But then again, so is Garth Brooks. I guess I'm surprised that "images" go beyond the music. I've been told this is a little naive. But sometimes when you're "in," on the road playing and singing, you forget that the playing and singing is still only a part of what Joni Mitchell once sang about as "the star-maker machinery behind the popular song." That machinery includes the obvious people—the record companies, artist management, bookers, promoters, and the like. There's also the whole second tier—the press and the public relations people who do their best to feed stories to the press. The record companies maintain their own public relations staff, and most artists—myself included—have someone on retainer. So we're constantly churning information, coming up with new "angles"—that is, little tidbits of information the press might be able to turn into a story—finding new and different ways to keep our names and our faces in front of you.

Of course, it helps to remember that this amorphous body I refer to as "the press" is really a diverse group of individuals who are paid to come up with stories that are different from everybody else's stories. That's how you can say you don't like a song, say "Achy Breaky Heart," and end up reading about it for the next sixteen months.

People, fans, have this rather interesting relationship with artists. I think of myself as a fan—and I have been a fan for longer than I have been a singer. I want my heroes to be a certain way. That makes it very easy to pigeonhole a person. I never really thought about that until I became a performer, and I discovered that it can be a multiple-choice test.

I am a:

a) a new traditionalist
b) a modern honky-tonker
c) a bluegrass kind of guy
d) the kind of man who beats his horse
e) all of the above

Country music has become a little like professional wrestling. Performers assume a persona, and then we all respond to the persona. I hear artists out there shouting, "Not so! Not so!"

Right.

I don't need any more negatives than I already have. I don't like being pigeonholed, and people don't like that; it makes me "hard to deal with." I pay attention to my business, and that hasn't increased my popularity much—"What do you mean, he read the contract?" And my music is different.

"I'm Gonna Be Somebody" started it, but what kicked the door completely open was "Put Some Drive in Your Country." It wasn't a radio hit, because it didn't fit into the "format" that everybody was playing out there. The song sold a lot of albums, to a new audience who hadn't heard that side of me yet.

Being able to relate to the audience is where it's at—good songs. You can play with your image all day long, back and forth, outlaw, rebel, romantic, balladeer, whatever you want to do, but if you don't have good songs, it's all going to amount to, as Charlie Daniels once said, "a nickel's worth of warm piss." *Find out what your fans want to hear and give it to them every time you play.*

You want to talk rebel? Willie Nelson told me the hard, cold facts—anytime you do things your way, you're gonna have to fight the establishment. Record label people who say it's not commercial; radio station research people who say it's not our format.

If you're gonna do things differently, you're gonna have to stand up to that. You've got to know your audience and trust that they're going to buy it when you're done.

I have always believed in doing things my own way. If I have to die by the sword, I want to be holding it before I fall on it.

And that makes everything about ten points harder.

I played a big concert in Jersey, sell-out crowd. Did my normal show, the same type of show I do every single night, and did not make one reference to Billy Ray Cyrus or "Achy Breaky" anything. One of my songs, "Outlaws Like Us," has one line in it that says, "You can talk all day about the next Billy Ray, but I'll cast my vote for Hag."

I could have said, "You can talk all day about the next Marvin Gaye," but I didn't figure too many George Jones fans would relate.

Next day on the radio, while we're heading to another show, I get to hear about the "ongoing controversy." Lighten up, guys, the sincere disk jockey told his listeners, including me, "You're like two little kids in a sandbox."

It's a big game out there. But God only knows, if country music was still just twang, twang, twang, I wouldn't have a career. So it's good the umbrella has opened up and encompasses this wide range of different styles. I think it's real cool, as long as the music is good. The thing I try to keep in mind is how much of this stuff is going to be around for as long as the Eagles work, or Merle Haggard, or George Jones, or Waylon and Willie. How many of today's fans are going to pull one of today's top CDs out of their collection in ten years and play it again and again. Kind of reminds me of the *Saturday Night Fever* soundtrack. I bought it, along with everybody and his brother. It was a monster. But I don't ever pull it out and listen to it anymore.

I don't even think I could find it.

On the other hand, I still pull out my Eagles "Hotel California" album and my Waylon "I've Always Been Crazy" album. Over and over. Because it's music that lasts—it was good then, and it's good now.

Me with Waylon Jennings. *(Photo by Rick Diamond.)*

Chapter 29

❀ ❀ ❀ ❀ ❀ ❀ ❀

Video Reality

The first time director Jack Cole suggested doing the video of "Anymore" in a Veterans Administration hospital, with me portraying a wounded Vietnam vet, I thought even though he was a great director, Jack was nuts. "Anymore" was a *love* song.

I didn't want to do a video of "Anymore" because I felt that the song stood so much on its own. I thought we might be doing too many videos—I had done five. So I was wanting to hold off.

Warner Bros. was very insistent, though, and I finally caved in.

"Send me a treatment from a producer that just knocks my socks off, and I'll do it. Otherwise I won't."

Videos happen in a lot of different ways. Because I write most of my own material, I'm way too close to the lyrics, the thoughts and ideas that I had when I wrote the song, to come up with something objective or different. It's fair to say that I already have a video of every song I've ever done, running in my head. And it's pretty much impossible to change.

We take a song that we agree to do a video of and shop that song to several video producers, asking them for their ideas on the video. We get treatments, which we pore through, trying to decide if this story or that story works. This is one of the hardest things for me, because of that video in my head. It requires me to be divorced from the song, to take that one step back and see the whole project.

I got several treatments that I didn't care much for. I was in Orlando, Florida, on vacation, when I got a Fed Ex package at the hotel. I grabbed it on my way out to eat. I was sitting in the restaurant when I started reading the treatment. I almost broke into tears reading the thing.

It was the story of a veteran, not necessarily Vietnam, very much in love. There's scenes of him with his wife, having a great time being together. The next shot is him in battle; there's a huge explosion and you hear screams of pain. He wakes up, and you realize it's all a dream, part of his ongoing nightmares. He's paralyzed. He feels like he's half the person he was before, and he's really having a tough time dealing with what's going on in his life. His wife is sending him letters and he won't take them; he won't take her phone calls; he won't accept her coming to visit him. He just doesn't want anything to do with anybody.

I started reading all this stuff, and I thought, "Man, this is powerful."

I decided the risk was worth it for a number of reasons beyond artistic merit. Vietnam is a long way away for me—as the rock group Poison sings, "In a time I can't remember, from a time he can't forget." For better or for worse, my images of Vietnam are shaped by movies—*The Deer Hunter, Born on the Fourth of July, Apocalypse Now*—not by the reality. And I think I share my generation's fascination with that time period, a fascination that can only belong to kids who never had to make the tough decisions that earlier generation did.

The director insisted on shooting in a real VA hospital, using as few actors as possible. I agreed, with all kinds of reservations. I've never been in the service, certainly never been in combat or shot at, never come back to a world that didn't give a damn. My first concern was that we have absolute respect for all the people involved. They're the ones who paid a price.

Secondly, I wanted to be honest in my portrayal. And the men helped me tremendously. In the week we spent shooting that video, I learned a year's worth of lessons. I heard personal stories about the war, funny stories, touching stories, horror stories. The men were so happy that anyone was focusing attention on them.

I guess no one realizes that, hey, they're still there, men who served with honor and are now warehoused, overlooked.

The video changed me.

When you're in the public eye, you get literally dozens of requests a day for contributions for very valid, very good causes. But it's important, I think, to have an effect where you can, to actually change something.

Since the video, I've been visiting VA hospitals across the country, and I want, more than anything else, to increase the public's awareness of these forgotten men and women. A donation of time or money means so much. I can't even really imagine what it must have been like, and how, twenty years later, the war is still going on. Nobody wants to see a bunch of guys in wheelchairs going down the street. That's the ugly side. Nobody likes to see that. But it's a problem, and it's out there, and if I can do something in any small way to just make people aware of that, I have to try.

Chapter 30

❀ ❀ ❀ ❀ ❀ ❀ ❀

Sophomore Jinxes

Album number two scared the hell out of me. Call it the sophomore jinx. Call it the incredible disappearing artist. Next time you're in your favorite record store, look at all those great first albums that were never followed by a great second album. The Christopher Cross syndrome—release one huge album, win a garageful of awards, and spend the rest of your career trying to figure out what happened.

"So, Travis . . ."

I was sitting in the record company offices while a mixed lot of executives dropped by.

". . . is the second album going to be as good as the first one?"

No. Actually I'm planning a complete album of

Gregorian chants set to a steel guitar. I got asked that question a million times. They never asked the second part of the question, but it was still there, hanging in the air like the smell of yesterday's cigars. ". . . or are you just a flash in the pan?"

I was having trouble being taken seriously. A lot of it was the "novelty song" question. Was "Country Club" a novelty song?

The second reason was the "ballad problem." Three of my hits had been love ballads. Would I be taken seriously as a balladeer when people knew I had a rock and roll edge? Anybody want to try angels on the head of a pin?

It came down, once again, to a question of categories—can we take him seriously if we don't know what category to slot him into?

I tried to put all the nonsense behind me and not think about it, but that's a little like trying not to think about the word "elephant."

I thought we had some solid potential. "Here's a Quarter" had been playing well on the road for over a year. I didn't know if it would be a monster hit, but I knew in my heart it would be a hit. "Someone for Me" was working well, and I felt equally good about "It's All About to Change." Marty Stuart had come up with "The Whiskey Ain't Working," so I actually felt more comfortable than I was letting on.

More importantly, I wanted to rock, to push the limits a little bit. I sat down with my producer, Greg Brown, and outlined my ideas.

"I think we were a little tentative with 'Country Club,' " I said. "Because we had to be."

I suggested we cut the country stuff knowing it's going to get country airplay, and let's cut the harder, more rock-oriented stuff knowing it's a risk. Maybe we'd pick up some airplay on the album-oriented stations.

A record producer has one of the hardest jobs in the business. A producer's job is to *hear* each song in a way that might be different from the singer's or songwriter's, to highlight the singer's and the song's strong points.

The actual recording went easily. Once we had the album, we had the coin toss of what to release as the first single. The big hot potato was "Here's a Quarter."

You can't risk, I was told, another novelty song. There was that word again—*novelty*. There were people in Nashville who thought a novelty song was any song that didn't have "deep meaning." There were also people in Nashville who thought a novelty song was anyone they didn't write. If you ask me, "One-Eyed, One-Horned, Flying Purple People Eater" is a novelty song.

Record execs are scared of novelty songs because neither the song nor the artist who sings it get taken seriously. There was also no shortage of theories about what to release as a first single—about the same number of theories as there are on how to make a hit record. They're all about equally correct, too.

"You'd be crazy to come on with a slow song for a first release, because it just doesn't . . . grab . . . an audience."

"Up-tempo songs are out. The market today's going for ballads."

"Medium tempo, something waltzy."

"Quarter" just felt good to me. My only concern was that I set the song up in performances: "Folks, I want to talk to you about marriage. People ask me all the time, am I going to get married again? Well, no. I've decided never to get married again. See, I've been married and divorced twice. Instead every five years I'm going to go out and find a woman I can't stand and buy her a house."

Got a big laugh. "But I wrote a song that tells a little bit about how I feel about marriage." As soon as I hit the hook line, everybody went crazy.

I should have known better, because a good song doesn't need an explanation. I always hated that, going to songwriters' showcases, where there's a guy on going, "This is a song that I wrote about my relationship with my mother just two weeks before she died, and this is what she said to me about life in general, as far as relationships, love, marriage, and the environment are concerned. If you pay attention to the words of this song, you'll realize that mothers understand a whole lot about love and relationships as well as the environment."

An old songwriter named Frank Dycus told me once that if you've got to explain the damn thing, you've got no business singing it to start with.

A nervous group of people, including the artist, put that record out. I wasn't nervous about it until they started being nervous. Once they were nervous, I thought, oh shit! If I make the wrong call here, I'm in a heap of trouble, since my deal was I get to call 'em until I make a mistake.

Made me nervous as the proverbial cat in the roomful of rocking chairs.

Driven by the success of "Here's a Quarter," the album went platinum in just a few months. I'd beaten the sophomore jinx. I wasn't a flash in the pan. Every single we released from that album went on to become a number-one record.

The single "Anymore" was on the top of the charts, and I was on a plane to California looking forward to the Super Bowl when I landed. I was on my way to the American Music Awards show in L.A., where I was nominated for an award. There were two scheduled country performances—Wynonna Judd and Garth Brooks.

I got off the plane and raced through the airport, trying to pick up as much of the game as I could from various monitors. I figured I'd get to the hotel at just about halftime, and slide from there. When I got to the limo, the driver had a different idea.

"Your manager called," the driver said. "You're going directly to the theater now to rehearse."

"Rehearse what?" I asked. "I'm not supposed to be there until tomorrow, when I get to say, hopefully, 'Thank you.' "

"Not anymore, sir," he said. "You're performing."

He rushed me to the theater, and I walked in and met Dick Clark, who thanked me for being able to fill in for Garth Brooks on such short notice. I just kept smiling and nodding, figuring that sooner or later I'd catch up with what was going on.

"What song are you doing?" Dick Clark asked.

Good question.

"Well, my band's not even here . . ."

"How about something acoustic?" Clark replied. "We've got a couple of big production numbers, LL Cool J and MC Hammer, with twenty, thirty people on stage. An acoustic thing would really stand out."

So I sat on the end of the stage in the middle of that show by myself and did "Anymore," one guitarist far in the background. That performance, in my mind, was one of the turning points in my career. I was noticed by people who never before listened to country, and I felt as if I had moved up to another plateau.

Chapter 31

❀ ❀ ❀ ❀ ❀ ❀ ❀

Double Platinum

One of the things about the business I've always found weird, extremely weird, is going on stage and being in front of seven, eight, nine, ten thousand people one minute, and five minutes later, literally, you're in a hotel room, alone, with nothing but silence all around you.

It's like being . . . cut off.

Taking one emotion as far as we can take it, and then just cut it off. No gradually easing out of it. Bang. Cut it off.

It's the weirdest feeling in the world, being in front of all those people, hearing the screaming and the roar of the crowd, feeling the energy and the adrenaline and all these different things, then, all of a sudden, to be back in a hotel room that is dead silent. Alone. Cut off from the outside world.

Anybody who can walk off of a stage after doing the kind of show we do, go back to the hotel, get in bed, and immediately go to sleep, you're a better man than I am. That's not my reality. That does not happen.

I can't write then, either. I just sit there and hum. Watch some lousy old movie I've seen before. Call some people on the West Coast (when I'm on the East Coast) who might still be awake. It's a very strange place, and it takes a while to learn how to deal with it.

I don't really remember my first big show, once we really hit. There was too much going on, too many miles on the road. I remember looking out and seeing a huge crowd of people, maybe it was Detroit or Jamboree in the Hills in West Virginia. It seems like I ought to remember that first big show, but it's lost to me now, scattered on the road like so much else. You're only as good as your last performance.

You can have a string of twenty dates, and the one that went wrong is the one you'll focus on, spend all your energy trying to figure out. There's an awful lot that can go wrong, with the crew, with the stage, with the sound, with the lights. With me.

My whole life I've always wanted so badly to give such a good show, such a good performance, that even if I don't feel like I've given my best, the crowd probably wouldn't know the difference. But I'll know. If I don't feel like I've given my best, I am very frustrated, and I tend to beat myself up more than I should. When that happens—and it does happen—I agonize over what can I do to keep that from ever happening again, and there is no way to keep that from happening ever again 'cause things are going to go wrong.

Murphy always wins.

The first year, after "Country Club," I did 280 days. That's just concert days, not counting video shoots, television show appearances, autograph signings at malls and record stores, recording sessions for the upcoming album, songwriting time, all the other details that go into keeping the business on the road.

I burned out on the road. Even though I had a great manager, and great booking people, great road people, I was the one generating the money. And the success and longevity of my career was going to rely on a lot of things, including my state of mind. I had to have balance. And no one is going to create that balance for you. You've got to create it yourself.

The music business is a money-generating business. A tremendous amount of money gets generated, and a lot of people rely on the salaries I generate. If I'm not able to go out and do the best that I possibly can do, then not only do I suffer, but we all do. And you can't burn yourself out. You're the only one who knows what your limitations are, and you have to set those up early and go by it.

Once you attain a certain level of success, there's a tremendous amount of pressure to go back and do it all again.

Not only duplicate it every night, but do better.

Once you get to the point where you're not doing better every night, or at least maintaining the same quality as before, then you start slipping off, and your fans start looking for the next new guy. It's just a fact of the business. If you manufacture a product of any kind, you have to consistently keep that quality; you have to have quality control.

If you don't have the quality, you drop off. Harley Davidson is a perfect example of that.

People quit buying them after they were sold to the huge sporting goods conglomerate AMF. Company went to hell in a handbasket. Damned near lost it. Now it's an American classic.

I think you lose track sometimes. I don't think you can have business goals—you can't say my goal is to have a number–one record. A number–one record is a side effect of producing good songs. They go hand in hand with each other.

It all comes back to the songs. Everything else follows.

It's easy, though, to confuse the business side with the artistic side. It's the difference between sitting down to write and thinking, "I want to write a good song," and sitting down to write and thinking, "I want to write a hit song." I've got to write a song for every album that has the impact of "Here's a Quarter."

It's not going to happen. Regardless of who you are, or how good you are, you can't nail it every time. If you allow yourself to be under that kind of pressure, you will methodically grind away your creative side. It's kind of like that Zen saying, "If you search for it, you can't find it." Or something like that. You can chase commercial success all over the place, and it will always be just beyond your reach. Which is easy to say or write, but that doesn't make the pressure go away.

I want to be successful for as long as I possibly can,

but I'm also realistic enough to know that every album I create is not going to sell two million copies, three million copies. It's not always going to be that way. And I have to resign myself to that. Unfortunately that's the way the music business keeps score. Not selling enough records? Out the door you go. They did that to Johnny Cash, one of the greatest artists in the history of country music. And they'll do it to me.

How much did it cost us to keep this artist on our label this year? Did it pay dividends? Was it worth it? Was it worth what we put into it? If the answer is yes, then you keep your label. If the answer is no, you don't. You're like a salesman on a quota. You meet your quota, fine. If you go above your quota, then you take your commission, and you can move along to the next year. If you don't meet your quota, the company finds someone who can.

But when I write, I don't—can't—allow myself to think that way.

But I do feel it creeping up on me.

After my albums having the success they've had— the first album out of the box, a million and a half; the second album, two million plus—the pressure is on for the third album to somehow do four million or five million.

I walked into the studio to start cutting T-R-O-U-B-L-E, and I violated every rule of my own that I've laid down here. I felt the heat, and I responded.

When we were planning T-R-O-U-B-L-E, Garth Brooks had dominated the charts with by far and away the most records sold. I was the number-two-selling artist.

I'd go into meetings, and we'd all look at those sales

figures, and sometimes my stomach would knot up. Somebody would always say, "Man, think about what the next one's going to do. Monster-monster."

Monster-monster.

Monster on my back. When we started putting together the T–R–O–U–B–L–E album, that monster-monster kept nibbling away at the back of my head. Is this as good as . . . We need another "Quarter" . . . Maybe I can write something really hot . . . If I'm not rising, I'm falling . . .

T–R–O–U–B–L–E shipped gold, has now sold a million and a quarter, well over platinum.

"I failed," I thought. "They all trusted me, and I stepped up to the plate, swung for the bleachers and missed."

A platinum album, forty weeks in the top 100 on the charts, a solid money-maker, and I'm walking around like my puppy got run over by a truck. It took some good friends to sit me down and give me a talking to, which is a little like having the shades lifted.

What was I thinking?

Why was I beating up on myself and the people around me?

Because of the difference between an artistic and a commercial hit.

The great thing about albums is they keep on selling. Whenever I release a new record, hopefully I get some new fans who've never heard of Travis Tritt before. They've just "discovered" me, and they're going to go back and find those old records. I did that with Hank, Jr., I did it with Waylon, I did it with Willie, I did it with the Allman Brothers—go back and buy. If you do a good album, it will never go away. People will rediscover you constantly.

It still comes back to those good songs. There's that constant push from inside the label; "You're making money; make more." Not to mention the band and road crew and their families who rely on me for their salaries.

And you can't help but respond to that push. But in the end, you have to do music you feel good about, music that feels comfortable to you. And if you can walk away from that studio before the album is released with the feeling that you did your best work, then whether it sells 25,000 copies or ten million, you'll feel good. I'll be proud fifty years from now to have that on tape. I didn't prostitute myself, didn't give in and do something that wasn't me. I did the best job that I knew how to do. Judge it that way.

Me with Marty Stuart and our Grammy Award.
(Photo by Jim McHugh. Used with permission from the National Academy of Recording Arts and Sciences, Inc.)

Chapter 32

Marty

a lot of good things came as a result of "It's All About to Change." Not the least was the beginning of my relationship with that guy in the flashy clothes, Marty Stuart.

Marty and I had met backstage at the CMA awards show my first year there. When I say we ran into each other, I mean it literally—two seconds. Marty had been around forever, but he was just starting to get the recognition he deserved, with songs like "Hillybilly Rock." When we partially collided, I said, "Hey man, I really like your stuff."

"I like yours, too," he said. "I really mean that, although I heard that you were a cod ass."

"That's funny," I said. "I heard the same thing about you."

That might give you a hint that Marty is tracking to his own drummer, and that drummer's so weird I thought I'd march right along. A few weeks later, my producer got a tape from Marty. A few nights later he showed up on the road one night, tape in hand.

"You gotta hear this one, Travis," he said. "You're gonna love it."

I did, of course. It was such a great song, I called him up and asked why he didn't record it himself?

"Just out of room," he said. "I already had thirteen songs for a ten-cut album."

I decided it had to go on my next album, and that it'd be a hoot to have Marty in to play the guitar part. While we were sitting in the studio, just clowning around, Gregg Brown got the idea to have Marty sing. Marty didn't want to, but after the appropriate whining, he agreed.

At first, he just sang harmonies, which those ex-bluegrass boys are good at. Gregg said try a verse, and Marty agreed. Next day, Gregg sent me two copies of the song, one with just me singing, the other a "duet" with Marty.

"Which do you think?" his note read.

No contest. Marty Stuart and Travis Tritt were destined to be the Wilburn Brothers of the 1990s. He's got the clothes for it, too.

"The Whiskey Ain't Working" hadn't even come out yet, and I was playing a series of shows during Fan Fair at the Opryland Geo Theater. Marty just happened by to wish me luck with the show, and I said, "Since you're here, why don't you come out and do 'Whiskey'?"

It didn't take much whining on my part this time. He agreed. Since the single hadn't been released, I wasn't expecting a wild response—audiences generally don't go crazy over a new song, and the only way they'd have heard it was if they'd purchased the album. Marty walked onstage unannounced when that song started; I didn't say a word. And the place just erupted. I remember looking at Marty, and his eyes were about as big around as silver dollars. Mine were, too.

Next time we got in touch with each other, we had some serious talkin' to do.

"Did you feel what I felt?" I said.

"Yeah," Marty said. "Have people been coming up to you all week at Fan Fair talking about that performance?"

"Yeah," I said.

"Maybe we ought to talk about taking this on the road," he said.

"And release 'Whiskey' as a single and do a video, while we're at it," I tossed in.

We got ready to do the video, and we knew there'd be no playing it straight. What you see on screen, two guys clowning around, having a great time, is exactly what happened. Between shoots, we'd go out to the bus and talk. I realized that Marty Stuart, in addition to being one of the most knowledgeable people in country music, was a kindred spirit. He's a brother. And I loved his stories about the old artists in country music, which is good, since Marty's been around forever and is constructed largely of stories.

Marty and I did *Nashville Now*, the Nashville Network talk show with Ralph Emery. While we were getting ready to go on, Marty told me about this article he had been reading in *Country Music* magazine about the huge wave of new country music, the invasion of the cowboy hats. And they showed pictures of Alan Jackson and Garth Brooks and Clint Black and Mark Chestnut and all these other people.

"Name two people missing from this picture," I mused out loud.

"You know what your problem is?" Marty said.

"Enlighten me," I replied.

"Exactly the same as my problem," he said. "We don't fit into one category. We don't have a nice little package you can put us in to draw attention to us. These guys all wear cowboy hats, pressed shirts, and starched jeans four inches too long that wrinkle up at the bottom. They look like rodeo stars. That's their gig, and we've got to come up with one of our own."

We started talking about it on the air, how to distinguish us from the "hat acts." I thought of calling us the "hair acts," but Marty thought that sounded too unsanitary. A few days later, Bonnie Gardner, Marty's manager, came bursting in with an idea she'd worked out with Ken Kragen:

What about a logo with a cowboy hat with a Ghostbusters circle and slash over it? Get it? No Hats.

"That's it," Marty said. "The No Hats Tour rides!"

"We're there, dude."

I figured, it's funny, maybe a speck controversial, but, hey, everyone can take a joke.

Garth Brooks at his press conference before his television special, when asked about the Stuart/Tritt "No Hats" tour:

"I just don't get it. I don't know what they're trying to do or what they're trying to say." While Garth was explaining about the Zen of Hats, the phone rang. It was Marty, congratulating me and himself on achieving "instant credibility." Next stop, the *National Enquirer!*

The tour was a roaring success, from the first dates in Alabama to the sold-out, 18,000 seat pay-per-view show in Knoxville, Tennessee. It was electric, and as much fun as I've ever had out on the road. We were one of the top-grossing tours of the year, and there are still about a million "No Hats" stickers stuck up all over America.

There are certain people you come in contact with who are tied to your life. More than acquaintances. More than friends. Truly bonded spirits. Marty is definitely one of those people. He's my brother, and I love him. And by the way, Garth, Alan, Mark, Clint and I get along with each other just fine.

From the video for "Anymore." *(Photo by Don Putnam.)*

Chapter 33

❋ ❋ ❋ ❋ ❋ ❋ ❋

...Put Me in the Movies

𝒲e all have those things in our careers that we have to apologize for.

Everybody does. Talk to actors, and they'll all tell you about some movie they did at the very beginning of their careers that they would just as soon never be shown anywhere, period.

I hope I've avoided that syndrome in *Rio Diablo*, my acting debut. At least it was a Western. There weren't any giant bugs or aliens, and all the women kept their shirts on.

I enjoyed acting, mainly because people ask me what my goals are now, now that I've had all this stuff happen for me? And that's a real tough question to answer, because all I ever wanted to do in my entire life was be a country music singer. It's all I knew how to do. And I still don't know how to do anything else the way I know how to do music. My dreams and ambitions and everything were fulfilled in a much bigger way than I ever dreamed possible.

And it's tough to go out and find new goals once you've had so many good things happen. But I believe it's even more dangerous not to have a goal. It's too easy to fall into the "same old, same old" habit. A new challenge keeps you fresh.

For me, acting is that challenge, because I knew right off the bat, from the very beginning, that I was not going to be a Robert De Niro. I can walk on stage, without getting nervous about performing, and I don't care how many people are out there, 'cause I know I know how to do that. I don't get any more nervous walking out on the stage in front of 60,000 people than a mailman does when he makes his route in the morning. It's my job. I know how to do this.

Acting is a different deal. I have to reach way down inside and challenge myself to do something I find very, very hard. I didn't even do a high school play, and I'm pretty sure that, no matter how good I get, I'm unlikely to be enshrined in the next *Gone with the Wind*.

Nevertheless I want to be as good as I can possibly be. Consequently I sometimes look at the tape for *Rio Diablo* and cringe. I wish I could've done that over again! But, hey, my character grew and progressed as the movie progressed, and I got better—I probably could not have gotten worse.

Wait—hurry up and wait.

When you're in the music business, things actually

move on a pretty regimented schedule, determined by the inescapable fact that at 8 p.m. or 10 p.m., you've got to walk out on stage and start singing, or there's going to be a lot of very pissed-off people.

You have a show time; you go on stage at 10. That means we leave the motel at 7, we get to the venue at 7:30, do our first meet-and-greet with radio people, then meet-and-greet with our fans, then meet-and-greet with our sponsors. Then I get ready to go on stage, do the show, go home.

For my first movie scene, I arrived on the set at 6:30 a.m. to do makeup. For a performer, 6:30 a.m. is a little hard—in fact, I'm not even sure it really exists. Suffice it to say I'm a speck slow at that hour. We were supposed to start shooting at 7:30 a.m.

No problem. Sit in the bus, read, talk to folks.

Nine-thirty. Watch some scenes getting filmed. Hang around with Kenny Rogers.

Sit in the bus, read, eat.

Twelve-thirty.

Sit in the bus, maybe get the makeup touched up.

Two-thirty.

Walk around sullenly, ask if this is always the way it works.

Three-forty-five.

Take a nap.

Five o'clock.

Get called to the set.

Five forty-five. Shoot first scene!

"Travis, we know you've done a lot of videos," I'm told, "but in movies, videos don't count."

I nodded agreeably. I thought they were nuts. I figure—and, granted, I'm a country singer—that when you have to get across an emotion without dialogue, that's acting. Well, they also wanted to remind me that I was on the set because of Kenny Rogers, who thought I'd made a pretty good on-screen cowboy. And besides, he'd already heard all the "don't counts" when he took the first *Gambler* role.

Ken Kragen had called me up, very enthused.

"For a start, it's not a *Gambler* movie," he said on the phone. Kenny had called him up, equally enthused. "It's going to be a big departure for me as far as roles are concerned, a completely different type of character, and there's a young character in this movie that would be ideally suited for Tritt."

"Man, I'd love to do it," I told Ken. Of course, I didn't point out that I had zero, zip, nada experience. Ken told Kenny, who went to CBS, who said, "He's got no experience."

Neither, Kenny pointed out, did he when he did the first *Gambler* movie.

"If you don't use him," Kenny said, "you'll be making a grave mistake. He's farther along than I was when I did *Gambler*."

The first day, when I had to shoot my first scene, everybody was sitting around holding their collective breaths. All I had to do was ride up to my fiancée's house the day of the wedding and give her a locket that belonged to my mother. And I'm not supposed to see her before the wedding, because she's a very strict Catholic and Spanish, and, if that's the case, you're not supposed to see the groom before the wedding. Or the groom's not supposed to see the bride. Or something like that. I defy all the rules and insist on seeing her to give her this locket.

I was a little nervous about the dialogue, because videos don't have a heck of a lot of dialogue. I had sort of envisioned an acting coach to get me through the worst parts. Right.

The most coaching I got was from Dolly Parton, who'd been interviewed in all these articles about how she'd impressed everyone on the set of her first movie by knowing not only her lines, but everyone else's lines as well. Okay, I'm a singer. I can memorize lines like there's no tomorrow.

The first day we did something called a read-through, where the principal actors and the director and producer and a bunch of other people I didn't have a clue about sit around the table and read through the script. You're not supposed to be "in character" at that point, which, of course, I didn't know. So I was.

I was all prepared, all revved up. Everybody else was sitting there reading the lines, and I'm *acting*. Everybody looked at me real strange. And then I saw Kenny start doing the same thing, and Kenny never does that.

Kenny is notorious for not reading scripts, much less reading them in character. He's the kind of actor who changes things on the set, who causes writers to get ulcers. On one of the *Gambler* movies with Linda Evans, just before the two were getting ready to do a critical scene, Kenny sat down and rewrote the entire scene, then took it to Linda Evans, who burst into tears. "How can you do this to me?" she said. "I'm not used to this sort of thing." No on-the-spot rewrites on *Dynasty*.

Kenny's got a very good sense of knowing what works—and how not to let his friends be humiliated at a read-through. And that helped me a tremendous amount, too.

They got me an acting coach, who I really appreciated, although I don't think I really understood where he was headed.

"Travis," he'd say. "Are you in your 'here' place?"

"No," I'd reply. "I'm in a 'there' place."

"What the hell is that guy talking about?" Kenny asked me one afternoon.

We shot the whole movie in three and a half weeks. It just so happened that I had blocked off a period of time right around then for vacation, so I had a working vacation in the desert at 114 degrees.

I liked playing a cowboy. Garth Brooks says he wants to play ax murderers. I think I'd be a lousy ax murderer. But I grew up on cowboy movies and watching *Gunsmoke* on television. Riding into the sunset—or snuffing Stacy Keach—is downright fun. Put on the Old West garb, got on a horse at the end of the day, and just rode through the old set. I actually felt like I was in the 1860s. It was very easy to get into that character.

I also learned the do's and don't's of the acting industry.

The big do is to do only what you absolutely have to do; the big don't is don't try to cover all the bases yourself. First day, I'd delivered my locket, and I was a Cool Dude, Mr. Actor Man. Excuse me, but where's my Actors' Equity card?

So I was watching them shoot an action scene, and my stunt double was in his forties, wearing a wig and a dyed beard.

He doesn't look a thing like me, I thought.

He had to fall off this wagon, and every time he did his wig fell off. After a couple of takes, Mr. Actor

Man—me—hitched up his jeans and walked over to the director.

"This just doesn't work," I said. "I mean, my 'double' doesn't look like me—nobody's going to believe that scene."

"You want to try it?" he said.

Uh-oh. "Well, yeah."

They got me all outfitted and ready to go, and the stunt guy gave me a quick little rundown:

I am thrown from a wagon and kicked in the face. Then, as I start to get up, I'm run over by a horse.

Hey, no problem for Mr. Actor Man.

So I climb up on the wagon and, on cue, heave myself into the street, which is very realistically covered with piles of horse manure, with the occasional cow patty thrown in for authenticity. I discovered when I hit the ground just how authentic. Then I was run over by a horse—which, by the way, never made the movie. There was lots of applause, which was almost covered up by the snickers. For four days, I felt just like I'd been . . . run over by a horse.

That didn't stop me from being stupid again. My next excursion into Stunt World ("Well, Travis, ready to do your own stunts again?") involved a lot of shooting over my shoulder. Then I got to stab a bad guy (not the director) and shove him into a fire.

The fire blazes up around him—that's what the script said. I didn't have sense enough to ask them to test it first. So I pushed the guy in the fire, and this roaring blaze does, in fact, come up around him. Me, too. It said the blaze singed off half my mustache, one of my eyebrows, and some of my hair. I got small first-degree burns up under my nostrils. I am not a stunt man. Big mistake. But I had fun. I got to play cowboy for almost a month and hang around a lot of people that I admire and respect. If I just had a chance to ride up and give my chosen that locket again—I think I understand the motivation now . . .

CBS told me they'd like to have me in other television productions, and I haven't pursued it simply because I'd like to aim for feature films. Something I learned from Kenny is if you plan to be in this business for the long haul, you have to find some way of layering your career with something more than just the music. Something that's going to keep you in the public eye after the music is gone. Otherwise you just dry up and go away. The music will change. It may take ten years, but the music cycle will roll around again, and the stars of today may not be the stars of tomorrow.

Kenny Rogers hasn't had a radio hit in forever. But he's considered to be one of the superstars of the industry because he is constantly visible—films, books, photography. And, you know, the other things will hopefully keep you in the public eye until the cycle comes back around and the music you're doing is popular again. And maybe you'll have another shot at it. Kenny has told me stories about being recognized on the street in New York City, not as a country music singer, but as "that Gambler guy." A lot of his fans don't even remember "that Gambler guy" started with that "Gambler" song.

I would like to do more acting if I get the opportunity, but right now music is the most important thing. That's the focus. It goes back to that old rule that my dad set—dance with the one who brought you to the dance. You do have to know when to hold 'em.

Chapter 34

✸ ✸ ✸ ✸ ✸ ✸ ✸

Willie's Birthday

Strangely enough, Willie Nelson's birthday party put a lot of things into perspective for me.

Marty Stuart came to my house just before he left to go on his tour recently, and he hung around for a few days. We hang around, act like Beavis and Butt-Head, watch country videos and trash everybody in fun.

"Ain't nobody worth a shit in this business except me and you," Marty joked.

"Yeah, and I'm beginning to wonder about you . . ."

But we watched the Willie Nelson sixtieth birthday television special—Marty hadn't seen the whole thing—and when the credits were rolling, I said,

"That was a cool thing. Meant a lot to me to be invited to be there."

It fit.

All those guys, part of the tremendous amount of influence I had growing up. Once again—good music, good songs.

I was pretty humble, pretty privileged to be sharing that stage with my idols. More like absolutely blown away.

I'd been walking by these heroes of rock and roll—Bob Dylan, B. B. King, Bonnie Raitt, people like that—all day long, people I'd never met before that I didn't figure knew me from Adam. In fact, people I didn't actually have nerve enough to walk up to and introduce myself.

I finished my performance, walked back to the green room, and Bob Dylan, B. B. King, and Bonnie Raitt walked up to me. One of the guys complimented me on my performance and shook my hand. I couldn't believe it, and I felt like for the first time I belonged. I was a part of something bigger than me, bigger than the honky-tonks, bigger than the road.

It reminds me of being backstage at the Grammy Awards, scrounging some food, when Eric Clapton came over to me, shook hands, and asked, "How'd the Buddy Guy song go?"

I think I answered something clever, like, "Okay."

I'd never met the man before in my life, but he is one of my idols, one of the few people I've ever met who makes my knees shake. The fact he even knew who I was astounded me.

I've always said I'm never going to be classified as a home run hitter. I'm never going to be the guy who causes you to say, "He's the greatest singer I've ever heard. He's the greatest songwriter I've ever heard."

What keeps me in the game, though, is the fact that I can play any position on the team and feel comfortable with it. I'll do a duet with George Jones, and then turn right around and do a duet with David Lee Roth and feel just as comfortable in both areas.

I think I realized how different my music was when Lynyrd Skynyrd asked me on stage for their homecoming concert at the Fox Theater in Atlanta. We did an unplugged thing before Skynyrd's set. It was me, Brett Michaels from Poison, Tom Kiefer from Cinderella, Charlie Daniels, Peter Frampton, and the guys from Skynyrd, each of us doing a different Skynyrd tune. I was at home, and I'm just as country as mud. But I don't just listen to country.

And I'm not the only one. Paul Overstreet, one of the greatest country songwriters ever, says it best, "I can't listen to country music very good."

We still seemed trapped in the "Hay Bale" syndrome that we're trying to overcome. I did a show not too long ago at Radio City Music Hall in New York City. My manager has always said you play every other city in the United States for money, but you play New York and Los Angeles for your career.

Well, I've played both places for years now, and though the crowds are large and seem to be having a ball, I have never gotten a good review out of either one of them. The critics say the same things about my stage and props—looks like something left over from the Rolling Stones' Steel Wheels tour. Or Megadeath. Darn, no wagon wheels and hay bales on the stage. How can I call this a country show?

I guess I could go out and change my show around to fit a different audience. But as a rule I don't. The first time I ever played in Indiana, I was opening for K. T. Oslin in a very nice, ritzy, velvet chair type place. K. T. was hot, and it was my first time ever in the market.

Ken Kragen came backstage right before the show, looking a little concerned.

"Have you looked out there and seen the crowd?"

"Nope," I answered. "Why?"

We walked to the side of the stage and peeked out through the curtain. The men were in their late fifties, and there were a lot of three-piece suits. The women were in long evening gowns like they were going to an opera. As a rule, I don't get a lot of suits and evening gowns at my concerts.

Ken said, "Travis, if you go out there and hit one of those loud chords on the Strat, some of these folks might cover their ears and run screaming for the exits. You might want to think about some last-minute changes."

"I can't do that," I told my manager. "That's going out and being something plastic, and something phony, something I'm not. It's giving the audience a perception that's not really true, and I think an audience will see through that."

And I went out and did my regular show. Luckily nobody ran for the doors.

You gotta take the whole package. And you can put it into any category or pigeonhole you want. But when I walked out on stage for Willie, I didn't have to worry about categories or pigeonholing. I knew when I was home.

Chapter 35

✿ ✿ ✿ ✿ ✿ ✿

The Road

The road from Marietta to Nashville rolls through the foothills of the Appalachian Mountains, through a world immortalized in thousands of songs. A hard world, one of hardscrabble farms, the soil leavened with rocks and the aging wreckage of a war the South will never forget. From the flatland of Marietta, the road climbs to around Monteagle, where you can watch the smoky mist rise in the mountains. From there it's downhill onto the Cumberland Plateau, into the flash and glamour of Music City. In the South, the old and new are tied together in a way that doesn't lend itself to explanation. Sometimes, when you're burned out from the road, trying to push those last few miles from home to work, the Civil War and the

Grand Ole Opry don't seem that far apart. No farther than the blues and soul. No farther than country and rock. *A thread, a melody, stretching back through the years . . .*

It's a strange world out there; it really is. And trying to stay one step ahead of the guessing game is an almost impossible feat. So you just go out there and do the best job you possibly can. Try to do good songs. Great songs. Hopefully, you'll last.

In Nashville, when you're hot, the idea is to do an album in November, finish it up, and immediately go out on the road and start touring to promote that album. Tour from November all the way until next November, and sometime during two weeks here and two weeks there, write an entire new album that's just as good, if not better, than the last one. Go in and record it in November, and do it all over again.

You can get caught up in this cycle, and it will absolutely rip you apart. You can't do it. In 1993 I shut that down. I said, "I'm not going to do an album. I'm not going to throw an album out there just to say I have an album out there. 'Cause once it's on tape, once it's pressed and on that CD, it's there forever. You can't take it back."

Some of the biggest songs that I've ever had in my career were songs that I wrote or co-wrote. That's a fact. For me to have the time to get those songs together, I have to get away from the road and be alone with my thoughts.

When I walk on that stage at night, that's the easiest thing I've done all day. I've talked with another one of my brothers, Gary Rossington from the Lynyrd Skynyrd band, about the difference between country and rock. A rock icon can lounge around all day until the limo comes to take him to the show, but that's not how we do it. We're accessible, and that accessibility of the artists and the music makes country what it is. So we walk a fine line between that accessibility and the necessities of image or mystique. Say whatever you want, but the fans don't want us to be one of the boys. They don't want us walking around backstage, wandering through the crowd. On what do I base that observation?

Me. I didn't want my heroes to be the guys or girls next door. I wanted them to be ten feet tall and bulletproof; to be, in at least some ways, larger than life. I wanted that element of surprise, of anticipation. What are they wearing? What are they going to sing?

In my own career, I strive for that balance.

I mean, ultimately, how many traveling musicians have a normal life?

My hat's off to people, first of all, who can stay married and, second of all, who can stay married and stay in this business.

There are very, very few of them out there—you can count them on one hand. *Dad or Mom is going to be gone for a month and a half, and I'll see you when I get home.*

Or you load 'em up, and here we go! That way, even though you're not in the same place, you wake up every day as a family. You do things together as a family. I think that's one of the keys to making it work. I'd like to see that happen. But on the other side, there is nothing in this world I can think of that's worse than to be married, have children, and have the marriage break up. That's a nightmare, and I would rather be dead than go through that. Unfortunately that's the risk; it's a roll of the dice.

A singer once told me the hardest part about being a traveling musician is having adult relationships, because you're not in an adult business, really. There's always the image of the star as a perpetual adolescent.

If you didn't have a childhood—or even if you did—you can have another one much bigger and better, because you can control it. You get bigger toys. How much maturity you're able to mix in there with it determines whether or not you're going to be successful in an adult relationship. There are tons of distractions out there, and it's very tough to stay focused. If I didn't learn anything else in both my relationships, I learned that to maintain a successful relationship, you have to work at it daily. And that's very tough to do with the road waiting right outside your door.

I honestly believe that an audience gets out of a show what they put into it. And the more energetic they are to start with when they come out there, and the more positive they are about what I'm doing— I'm not going to leave until I entertain this crowd. Not just sing for them, not just play them my hits.

When you go out with that kind of determination, and you just start feeding off that energy, all of a sudden you start getting it back. And it starts going back and forth, building each time. Before you know it, it's a big ball of excitement. And I think the crowd definitely feeds off it.

If you walk out there negative—why am I even doing this?—the audience picks that up right off the bat, and it kills the energy before it can really be born. It never gets off the ground.

That's why I say if you're not having fun, get out of it. My dad told me that, and he said it applies to everything in life. He told me that about a construction job I had, and he told me that about a girl I dated. So damn simple. "If you're that unhappy about what you're doing," he said, "then you got no business doing it."

I'm still learning. If I wasn't, what stupid things would I have to write about?

Me at Fan Fair.
(Photo used with permission from Celebrity Photo Agency.)

Chapter 36

❀ ❀ ❀ ❀ ❀ ❀ ❀

Epilogue

The highway rolls out of Albuquerque through the high desert, climbing toward the low adobe of Santa Fe. It rolls past Native American pueblos, baked as red as the desert earth around them, past tourist traps and silver-and-turquoise outlets, through a land that, through the vehicle of hundreds of cowboy movies, has become part of our shared mythology.

The highway skirts Santa Fe, heading through the mesas to a dusty rodeo ground in Arroyo Seco, not far from the rich and beautiful watering hole of Taos. But Arroyo Seco is about as far as you can get from Taos in another, more immediate way.

It's a rodeo ground like the ones I grew up playing, where some poor, beat-up band gets to play eight seconds, or until some equally poor, beat-up cowboy buries his face in the arena. For Arroyo Seco, that arena is a lifeline to a world away from the farms and the cattle and the roadside turquoise stands, where about the greatest thing a kid can imagine is walking through those rodeo grounds wearing the big silver buckle of a champion.

I'm walking through the rodeo grounds wearing the big silver buckle of a champion, but I didn't get it fair and square, on my face in the dust.

I got it from Property, like the jeans and the cowboy shirt—not even the dusty boots are mine.

The rodeo ground is surrounded by the immense paraphernalia of movie-making—cameras, huge booms, lots and lots of assistants with clipboards— another gold rush of tenderfeet from Los Angeles and New York, come to mine the great mother lode of "cowboy." I have a little speaking part in a movie called *Cowboy Way*, where cowboys will spit tabaccey and say, "Do hobbyhorses have hickory dicks?" If you can get over the endless hurry-up-and-waits, it's all great fun, if a little surreal. I could tell you about the "bronco-cam," designed to capture realistic images of a bucking horse from the perspective of the cowboy. Of course, the "bucking bronc" was actually a teddy-bear-soft, life-size stuffed horse's head, attached by a suspender-like mechanism to the chest of a camera-man. To capture the reality of a bucking bronc, the cameraman ran around backstage, bobbing up and down as if bucking, filming over the horse's ears. It was a promotional thing—go figure.

I'd spend most of the day on the bus, waiting for my thirty minutes in front of the camera. As I'm walking back to the bus, Woody Harrelson, one of the stars, comes rushing by and taps me on the shoulder.

"Let's pick," he says.

So we end up on the bus, the movie star with his old vintage 60s Epiphone guitar and me with my regular road Gibson.

It's late in the afternoon, and thunderstorms are rolling in over the mesas. Lightning lights up the horizon, and the brief rain has washed the skies clear of the omnipresent dust. You can learn an awful lot about people when you sit down to pick with them. Is it going to be a contest, a couple of dogs walking around in a circle sniffing? Is it going to be Guitar 101 or "Play me your greatest hits"? Or is it going to be for the love of the music, just to bend those strings?

We sat on the bus, storms flickering across the mesa, and harmonized on old Eagles songs, played some blues, picked some bluegrass, sang some of my songs and some of his songs. No crowds, no audiences, no pressure—just Woody's eight-month-old daughter laughing and dancing to the magic in the music.

From the rodeo grounds, you can see the highway, like the melodies in the songs, twisting, turning, but always going on. We have this deal with the road, those of us who travel it. Follow the road, touch the hundreds, the thousands of lives along the way, and there's fame and fortune there for the taking. Reach out, and the stories—the currency of the road—are also there for the taking.

I'm trying to keep it together, and it's damned hard. I mean, I want to say I'm the same person I've always been, but it's hard to sort through that when you pull into a town and there are a bunch of young women

215

outside your bus screaming "Travis! Travis!" I'm not complaining, mind you, but it's hard to keep your head bolted on the right way.

I take vacations back in Georgia, I keep up with my friends, and I listen to the music that's made me. I've said before that the thing about country music is it's the soundtrack to working people's lives, and I believe that. That's why country is the most popular music in America right now—because it connects to our everyday existence. People stand and cheer for "Here's a Quarter" because every darned one of them has wanted to say that once—to a husband or a wife or a boss or a whining relative. It connects. It's real. It's more than hype. Much more.

Funny thing, you know. When I can get away, I scuba dive, because it's a way into a different world. It's calm and quiet and beautiful. But I'll be down there in that different world, letting my cares just float away, and somewhere in the back of my mind, I'll hear a jukebox starting up. I'll be looking at some blue fish down in the Bahamas, and I'll hear George Jones or Merle Haggard. Or maybe I'll hear music I haven't heard before, music that I wish I had a way to capture before it slips away like that blue fish.

Or like the rush of air when I head down the road on the Harley, the sounds of the highway, the music of the wind.

Like Willie says, the music's everywhere, just waiting for us to write it down.